Poisoned By Pollution -
An Unexpected Spiritual Journey

By Anne Lipscomb

With Foreword by David Buscher, M.D., FAAEM
Former President,
American Academy of Environmental Medicine

authorHOUSE®

AuthorHouse™
1663 Liberty Drive, Suite 200
Bloomington, IN 47403
www.authorhouse.com
Phone: 1-800-839-8640

Cover illustration © 2008 by Eric Giriat
(www.ericgiriat.com)
Cover graphic design by Nicki Dausend
Author photograph © 2009 by Don Wilson

ISBN: 978-1-4389-6502-4 (sc)
ISBN: 978-1-4389-6504-8 (e)
ISBN: 978-1-4389-6503-1 (hc)

First published by AuthorHouse 4/10/2009

Printed in the United States of America
Bloomington, Indiana
This book is printed on acid-free paper.

Library of Congress Control Number: 2009902638

www.annelipscomb.com

This is a true story based on the author's experience and extensive notes she has kept throughout
her illness. All names have been changed except for that of the Department of Labor & Industries;
her attorney, Chuck Kimbrough; Adeleine Crinks of On the Job Injuries; the Dondey family; and
the Madkour family. Occasionally a person's physical description has been changed to obscure
his or her real identity. The author's intent is to recount her journey and not to embarrass anyone
or place blame. It is the story that is most important.

The information in this book is not intended as medical, legal or psychological advice. Any
theories, treatments, physicians, products or opinions mentioned do not represent endorsements
or recommendations, and do not take the place of medical, psychological or legal advice tailored
to specific individual conditions. Medical, legal and psychological advice should be obtained
from licensed professionals in personal consultations. Products and/or treatments that may be
effective for some people may be harmful to others. Any persons using products or treatment
modalities referred to in this publication, or who consult with or engage in treatment with any
person or agency referred to in this publication, expressly waive any claims they, their heirs,
successors or assigns may have now or in the future against the author or publisher arising out of
any cause of action that may be created by the use of said product or service.

Dedicated to
Loy Ann Carrington
and
Kathleen Lipscomb

When it is dark enough, you can see the stars.
                        – Ralph Waldo Emerson
All truth passes through three stages:
First, it is ridiculed; second, it is violently opposed;
third, it is accepted as being self-evident.
                        – Arthur Shopenhauer

Table of Contents

Acknowledgments

Because this book has been 15 years in the making, at times I have despaired that the project would ever be completed. Were it not for a team of people helping me during these years, I would not have been able to pull it off. No one writes a book alone, I've learned, least of all me.

Thomas Stuby served not only as an editor but also as a coach who showed me how to write a better book. Patricia Ochs came into my life as part editor and part fairy godmother with such generosity of spirit. She helped me with many things beyond editing. Constance Buchanan and Phyllis Hatfield edited the book in the earliest years. Diane Sears and Elizabeth Lyon have advised me throughout the trials and tribulations of the many tasks required to send a book out into the world. Dr. Eileen Allen served as a mentor who encouraged me to get started on the project, rather than just talk about it.

Additionally, so many others contributed toward shaping the book. For the sake of privacy, I will not name them. Some read my manuscript and shared their thoughts. Others helped me think through what I wanted to say. Chemically ill people told me their stories. Various professionals – from journalists to healthcare providers to contractors designing healthy buildings – allowed me to interview them. They have all played an important supporting role. Finally, since I've been ill throughout the project, a team of friends helped me by typing up my journal and interviews, copying materials, contributing ideas, bringing library books to me, and helping me with my computer.

I thank my entire book team, as well as my healthcare and legal team, and all the compassionate people in my life who have stood by me during difficult times, even when I haven't always been fun to be around; who have opened their windows during my visits, even in winter; who have changed to unscented shampoos and soaps; who have accommodated my ailing body in countless ways. You have all helped me enormously to have some quality of life despite the most challenging of circumstances.

Foreword

The Chemical Problem

Twenty-first-century living has brought major advancements in technology and science, which have resulted in many positive and beneficial changes. Unfortunately, there has also been a down side. Scientists and physicians are becoming increasingly concerned about the effects of thousands of chemicals we use daily. The past 50 years has exposed us all to a multiplicity of synthesized chemical compounds that previously had not existed before. Environmental medicine physicians are well aware of the implications of this chemical pollution and its effects on the patients they see.

Multiple chemical sensitivity (MCS) is somewhat of a recent medical phenomena. It is poorly understood and controversial, and doctors are finding it difficult to provide curative treatment. Those who have it show a very high degree of sensitivity to a diverse array of low-level chemical substances, which can cause a multitude of different symptoms.

Physicians who specialize in environmental medicine say the incidence of MCS is rising, and available data suggests this is the case. Estimates of the prevalence of MCS in the U.S. population are based on random studies of medical clinic patients, general populations and telephone surveys. One of the earliest studies, in 1987, suggested 2 percent to 10 percent of the population had developed chemical sensitivity. A study in 1999 estimated 15.9 percent of respondents had hypersensitivity to common chemicals. Studies from 1993 through 1996 estimate between 15 percent and 33 percent.

The cause of MCS and its rising incidence correlates with the introduction of an overwhelming diversity of chemicals we are all exposed to daily. Chemicals are ubiquitous and present in all areas of our life. We are born with toxic chemicals already in our tissues; and the longer we live, the more we accumulate. These chemicals are in our air, water, food, clothing, furniture and beds. Pesticides used in Texas find their way to remote areas such as the Arctic through a process known as "leapfrogging." We spend 95 percent of our time indoors or in cars, where chemical toxins are more concentrated.

MCS is only the tip of the iceberg when it comes to the "chemical problem." Chemicals that have been implicated as carcinogens and endocrine disrupters – substances that mimic the effects of hormones and play a role in hormone-related cancers of the breast and the prostate – are more prevalent today than ever. Products made from bisphenol A (BPA) and phthalates are found in polyesters, epoxy resins and polycarbonate plastic, which means these chemicals are in our water bottles, food and beverage cans, sports equipment, household electronics, medical devices, dental sealants and more. Recent evidence links BPA with cardiovascular disease, diabetes and obesity.

Total avoidance of these chemical toxins is close to impossible. But the general population's awareness of the dangers these toxic chemicals carry is higher than it was 30 years ago. Industries are developing less-toxic building materials, effective air and water filtration systems, healthier cosmetics and personal-care products, and foods that are less contaminated by chemicals. Each of us has the ability to reduce our level of exposure by making informed and healthy choices about where we live and what we drink and eat.

Proper stewardship of this incredible planet earth calls for reducing the sources of toxic chemicals as much as possible. Perhaps this can best be achieved by grassroots dissemination of information about the chemical problem to our neighbors, schoolteachers, news media and elected leaders. Awareness of any problem is the first step in bringing about change.

Anne Lipscomb's book is a good example of a way to increase public awareness. Anne is a chemically injured woman whose life was greatly affected by toxic exposures at her workplace. She refused to give in and be defeated by such a tragic incident. Through her keen intelligence plus monumental effort, Anne was able to manage her condition and restore her life to some sense of normalcy, and then use her creative abilities to write this most important book.

Environmental medicine offers a sweeping reinterpretation of medical thinking; especially its approach to many previously unexplained and ineffectively treated chronic diseases. The basis of this view is the simple concept that there are causes for all illnesses, and the obvious – but not well-accepted – fact that what we eat or are exposed to in our environment may have a direct and profound effect upon our health. The goal of environmental medicine is to identify the cause of a health problem and eliminate or reduce the level of exposure as much as possible.

The increase of environmental chemicals is having subtle, yet far-reaching effects on the health of the population of America and the world. More research has to be done into the cause and treatment of environmental illness. There is much debate among traditional and environmental medicine physicians today. The patients are caught in the middle. We all need to work together to prevent environmental illness – and we can start by leading lives that are as non-toxic as possible.

David Buscher, M.D., FAAEM
Former President
American Academy of Environmental Medicine

Introduction

I write to you from the perspective of illness. Sickness imposes limitations. They alter but they need not define me. My perspective, as a result, is a hopeful and enlarged one.

For a long time I used to go to bed feeling as if I lived in a prison. My chemical illness had closed off my world. This illness no longer writes my life. I have become my own author. The story of how this came to be is one I want to share. This book is not just a re-telling of my illness. It is also the story of how I came to be this new person, with a newly expanded expression of my soul, and then, a writer of my life.

Writing this book while sick has been a challenge. I've spent too many days and too many years lying in bed feeling like poisons were coursing through me. For years, I could not even read or write without growing dizzy and nauseated. Sometimes I would talk into a tape recorder instead. Or I would write a few sentences, then close my eyes until the dizziness and nausea subsided before continuing on. At one point I almost died when my digestive troubles worsened so much that I couldn't hold down food or water, which led to my body being in a starvation state with my organ systems shutting down. The road to this book has been long indeed.

This book has been 15 years in the making. When I first fell ill 16 years ago, several friends suggested I write a book about the experience. I found the idea crazy, sometimes even irritating. I felt as if I were standing helplessly, watching my house become engulfed in flames, while friends sat by and talked about how I would write a book about it all. I am just trying to survive, I would tell them. I am not a writer.

Gradually, though, I became astounded by the number of people suffering from various forms of chemical-related illnesses. For some, their lives had become a living hell, invisible to the world. I came to see that chemical-related illnesses were one of the biggest public health problems of our time. Very little was being done about it. So I started warming up to the idea of writing about it. I wanted to give a voice to an issue that has lived in silence for too long. I thought my story might be easier to tell because I fell ill so suddenly and the cause was obvious. One month I was living and working in Seattle with a full and rich life. The next my life had collapsed around me and I couldn't do simple activities of daily living. For many, however, the damaging health effects of chemicals build up slowly and quietly over many years. Then one day, like cancer, it can come out of the blue, leaving one to wonder how it could have happened.

What began as a book about my illness widened to include the personal and spiritual journey it sparked in me. My sickness has radically changed me. It has altered the way I live in this world.

As the *doing* side of my life receded, however, the *being* side increased. This transformation has been just as much a part of my story as my physical afflictions. In fact it is certainly the best and most remarkable part.

I can write only about my experience. Someone else put under similar circumstances might draw different conclusions, might live differently, might write a different sort of book. We each bring a unique life and person to something disrupting like an illness. One response is not necessarily better or more right than another.

If someone had told me in the first 10 years of my illness that I would eventually arrive at the place where I now find myself, I would not have believed it. To be honest, I did not think myself capable of it or this book. But illness has taught me what I am capable of doing. Perhaps illness is the doctor to whom we must pay heed. I have come to see that misfortune can come to be one's spiritual awakening. The story of this making is what I offer you now.

Anne Lipscomb

Reflections upon my personal and spiritual journey can be found on pages 73-77, 96-98, 120-121 and in the chapter An Unexpected Spiritual Journey, which begins on page 163, and the Afterword, which begins on page 177.

Reflections upon relationships with long-term illness, and how to maintain them, can be found in the chapter The Biggest Challenge of All, which begins on page 128.

PART I

ILLNESS

Worlds that Shatter

I smell a croissant and suddenly I am 20 again. When I take the first bite, its crisp exterior shatters into tiny, layered, individual worlds, which transport my body and mind into some distant dream. Its subtly rich aroma speaks immediately to me of some older world, one of elegant ornamentation. But it also offers an intense private moment of indulgence that has been so long in the making. The flaking croissant at this moment becomes an emblem for a sensuous life reborn.

Croissants were often weekend breakfasts for me when I lived with the Dondey family as a college student in Paris. I loved how their buttery perfume would curl up my nostrils and flow through my mind and body like a fragrant river. In Paris, I learned that a croissant could quickly become a lesson in sense experience and pleasure. As this young woman, intoxicated by the sensations of that city, I was constantly reminded that our lives are made up of such sensual moments, that we are complicated and restored by our sensual interactions with the world. It was that heightened sensuality of France that beckoned to me when I could first contemplate a holiday abroad after having lived housebound for 14 years – that and the chance to see the Dondey family once again.

I am standing in line at a bakery in Paris, astounded I've been able to make such a trip. My world has been barren for so long. I have been so bereft of sensory pleasures that every remembered detail now hurls itself at me until my head throbs like a drum beat: The aroma of fresh yeast mingled with newly baked bread and pastries drives me a little wild, the baguettes standing at attention in proud wooden racks, below them, the

3

pistachio escargot buns lined up like serene rows of seashells beneath the gleaming window of the case. I see this all so vividly now. The white tile floor is worn thin by the history of customers queuing up for their daily bread. A woman is standing in line ahead of me, with her child tugging at her skirt, begging for some special treat, it seems. They are chattering away in a language I have not heard in far too long.

I drink all of this in, as if I had been starving through a famine for 14 years, and then suddenly, I am brought to a rich brocade of a room, and in it a banquet table is laid out with sumptuous foods just for me. I want to hold this moment forever and never leave this spot. It remains so ordinary, so much of the daily routine, yet so very miraculous to me as well. I have missed moments like this and the heady stimulation of a place with so much texture. An unbridled joy begins in my mind and wells up in my throat. Tear pools gather in the corners of my eyes. I feel resurrected from the dead.

✑

I arrived in Paris originally as a junior in college, lugging my suitcase up a tall flight of stairs. I couldn't find the elevator because I was so nervous about meeting my host family for the first time. The door opened to my wide eyes, and before I could stammer out my pre-rehearsed introduction in French, Dr. and Mme. Dondey, along with their five children, spilled into the entrance hall from every direction. Immediately, they put me at ease, showing me to my room, and then teaching me how to make crêpes for dinner. That night I climbed into my bed grateful that I had come to France and hopeful for what my future there held.

My early Paris days became a pleasant ritual of attending classes scattered throughout the city, followed by evenings with the Dondey family. Dr. Dondey would arrive home from work around 8 p.m. He would slip on a velvet smoking jacket and we would gather for drinks in the living room. Dinner would follow as a kind of leisurely tourism: A multi-course meal was always thoughtfully paraded before me, which ended with a plate of various cheeses and a fresh sliced baguette. I have no idea how long we spent at dinner each night except that by the time we rose from the table, it was nearly time for bed, and soon the ritual would begin again. Looking back, I appreciate better the rhythms of this existence, the careful attention paid to smells and tastes. Life was a repetition of the senses, so to speak, but it was never boring. Little did I know then that in the future I would eventually lose hold of this simple, daily sensory feasting, and long for its return.

Beyond our daily forays into food and drink, my Paris life was a sensual feast in other ways as well. On weekends we sometimes piled into the car and drove to a movie on the Champs-Élysées. Or I might sit as a model for Dr. Dondey, who painted in his spare time, as Mme. Dondey read aloud passages from a Marcel Proust novel assigned to me in class, translating into English some of the passages I had trouble with. I remember one particularly vivid Saturday when we drove to the small town of Honfleur for the day, where we ate lunch at an outdoor restaurant, situated on a farm, with chickens bustling about beneath round tables draped with blue-and-white checkered tablecloths. Our table was set with thick white china and cloth napkins and our bottle of white wine sat chilling inside a silver bucket. We began the meal with a platter of oysters and shrimp and snails, and secretly fed bits of it to the Dondeys' dog underneath the table. Afterward we strolled into town and Dr. Dondey set up his drawing pad and charcoal pens on the stone wall that lined the waterfront to capture the light of the day, as the rest of us wandered around town, taking in its simple serenity. A faded white wooden sailboat lapped gently at the water's edge, basking in a mirror of water that reflected the rows of gray and white and ochre townhouses clustered like a necklace along the quaint harbor.

My year in France taught me so much about myself, my senses, food, art, and numerous other things. This was the year I sat in cathedrals for hours on end, researching Romanesque and Gothic architecture. It was the year I walked everywhere, more than I ever had in my life, for I was taken by the city's beauty and did not want to miss one bit of it. It was the year that awakened in me a love for food that would never leave me. It was the year I would repeatedly fall into bed, exhausted from the effort of speaking a language I had not quite mastered. But most importantly, it was the year I learned about the art of appreciation and its pleasures. Or rather, in France I learned the very art of appreciating pleasure – an art lesson that would, unknown to me at the time, become even more crucial to me later, and especially now.

I loved the way the French tended to savor the details of their daily lives, the way they valued the ability to appreciate something, to soak in its sensory richness. Pleasure was a priority to them. At least it seemed to be much more of one than it was in the United States. Slowly, as I found myself becoming more and more influenced by the French spirit of appreciation, it felt as if more pleasure was drawn into my days. The French seemed to find intense enjoyment from a wider spectrum of things: for example, the foods we typically pass by or the bits we normally throw out. That broader range even seemed to affect aspects of life like their relationships. In those days in France, you could be, say, a senior citizen and still be seen as attractive or regarded as sexy. The French savored their romantic partners the way they appreciated their wines. Older wines had certain characteristics; younger wines had others. But there was much to enjoy about both. Such outlooks expanded the lens through which I viewed life, which led me to palpably feel the enjoyment of life more and more.

Looking back now, the experience in France is important for my story and what I have come to learn about my journey. It has made me more aware of how oriented we Americans have become toward work and self-improvement, rather than toward the more immediate pleasures of daily life. We often miss how quietly those pleasures seep into so many parts of our lives. Even though I had been exposed to the French orientation toward pleasure at a young age, before illness took me down I could tend toward self-improvement efforts and the achievement fever that often permeates American culture, whether it was in my work life or when trying to get my body into athletic shape. It would take a major sickness to make me realize that while my self-improvement endeavors had produced some fine results, the balance had been tilted too heavily toward bettering myself and making future goals, and not enough on simply feeling joy and finding pleasure in the moment. Also, I saw how too much of an emphasis on self-improvement had made my days busier and sometimes more stressful, and it tended to make me focus on what I wanted to achieve rather than savoring what I already had and the life that was passing by. Memories of my time in Paris then trickled back and reminded me there was another way. It was as if my Paris experience had been sitting on a dusty shelf somewhere in my memory, waiting for a period when I had ample time for reflection and enough maturity to more fully digest and learn from the experience.

Wonderful memories of living with the Dondey family decades ago came rushing back to me, when, on this trip back to France, I had lunch with their youngest son, Laurent. I sat with Laurent and his family at a sidewalk table outside of a small restaurant along the St. Martin canal. Laurent and Nicki, with their two-year-old, Alma, had chosen the Hôtel du Nord not only for the view, but also because there is a famous French movie named after the restaurant and much of it was filmed there. The day was gray and damp, yet surprisingly quiet because no car traffic was allowed in the neighborhood on Sundays. Even though it had been ages since I had seen him, those passing years seemed to melt away, as if we were back in our youthful Paris.

In a way, having lunch with an old friend seems like such a normal event, but I will never forget it: not the jade green pedestrian bridges arching over the canal, not darling Alma stretching out her little hand to me so I could hold it while we visited the kitchen just to satisfy her curiosity, not the lively conversation we had comparing our respective cultures, not the taste of arugula and sun-dried tomatoes dancing in my mouth. The scene was exhilarating and surreal. While a part of me was discussing politics with Laurent and Nicki, another danced high above the scene, nearly out-of-body. I seemed to move to a chorus singing out to me that I was whole again. It wasn't just the dream I had been having of regaining my former self. It seemed to be happening. A similar chorus in my head would serenade me throughout the holiday, and by the end of my trip, I had come to believe it. It seemed ages since my health troubles had severed me from much of my self, especially from my adventurous and exploratory spirit, which delighted in traveling to far-flung destinations. For years I had lived like a wounded bird, limping about on one leg, unable to fly. My illness not only cut me off from a central pleasure but it also deprived me of seeing my friends abroad, which for me is one of life's best experiences. Sitting in that restaurant, I felt like I had whiplash, going from such a confined life to having lunch with Laurent and his family as if this was an ordinary day.

Part of me had been in this city before; but part of me had not, at least not in this way. It was as if I had been deaf the last 14 years, with no hope for recovery, and then all at once I could hear the singing choirs of life all around me. My senses had never felt so alive, my heart never so wide open to the world. I felt like Rip Van Winkle, awakened after too long a sleep. All around me, rose petals seemed to be falling from the sky. I wanted to collect them, take them to my skin, and convince myself that I had been remade somehow.

"Laurent," I gushed, "I just have to tell you that a part of me cannot believe this is happening. For years, I thought I would never again visit this city, would never see old friends like yourself, let alone feel my body and mind rejuvenated in this way. I thought parts of my life were finished. I feel so grateful." Laurent smiled, as if touched by the thought. He didn't quite understand the enormity of my situation, what I have been through, or how this experience in Paris and all that it stands for in my mind became symbolic of so much of my transformation and my journey. My pain, in this moment, was countered by those sensory pleasures I rediscovered in the city of lights.

After my moment of rapture, we resumed our conversation. How could I articulate at this time that for me being back in Paris, this light-filled city where I once lived and had visited every few years until this tumultuous 14-year interruption of my illness, has felt like the test of my life. It represents where I long to be now, where my senses and the pleasures of life might be restored to me. It has shown me just how radically I have changed. I realize that though illness has taken much away, much still remains. On all of my previous trips to France, perhaps I'd altered or grown in small ways from one visit to the next, but the changes were too subtle to notice. This time has meant something else altogether. It is as if some new planet or bright star has appeared in sight.

How could I have known back then, in those early salad days of Paris, that my life would rupture so violently and completely, that I would never be the same as a result of it? And how could I have known that in some sense, I would end up different today in surprisingly wonderful ways as well? Part of me feels astonished by the unexpected life I've acquired, even by the fact that in this moment I know I will write a book about it all. I think about how little I know for certain about what lies ahead and that all I can be sure of is this moment of transport, memory and renewed health.

In many ways, I realize all at once that I want to tell my story about what it has meant to have been dropped out of normal life for over a decade and what that experience has taught me as I struggle to return, changed from what I once was. But I also realize I need to write about this because I know now that so many other people also struggle with a little-known sickness called multiple chemical sensitivity and other chemical-related illnesses. I am saddened by how many of us suffer in silence, and always under a cloud of suspicion. That's part of the suffering. I want to contribute by giving the illness a voice and a habitation. I want others to understand how I arrived at this point of view, this new way of perceiving the rhythms of life, in addition to how I came to be sick. I am lucky and at an advantage, in some sense, because I fell ill suddenly and the cause was obvious. Therefore, I can understand things more clearly. For many, however, the symptoms emerge so slowly and so subtly that over time it is difficult for them to see their connection to the everyday pollution and chemicals that inhabit the air or water around them.

❧

I stroll toward the Tulerie Gardens on one of my last evenings in France. On my way back to the apartment, I see an elegantly dressed violinist and harpist. They're playing a haunting melody beneath a stone archway of the Louvre. I stop and listen. The music is soaring through me and over me. I continue on, passing picnicking families on unfurled blankets and lovers sprawling on the grass, their bodies reposed and intertwined. Straight ahead, in the distance, the Egyptian obelisk at the Place de la Concorde is a glowing sentinel reaching for the setting sun. The grand and imposing Arc de Triomphe lies far behind it, anchoring the end of this axis that begins with the Louvre. I see it all, and in fact feel it all, as kind of a part of me.

My days in France have all been like this, drenched with the impossibly beautiful. The sights, sounds and smells of this city have meant so much to my spiritual journey. Ecstasy courses through me like a wild river spilling over its banks, with almost too much emotion to contain. All at once I need to retreat to a café to find a quiet, reflective moment. Visiting Paris has been like looking through a kaleidoscope of dazzling color shapes. Sometimes I am exhausted by trying to make sense of it all, even if my senses themselves can never be exhausted by this place. Being here has pulled up that heavy anchor holding me to my house, most often chaining me to my bed, where I have lived in a state of survival, just trying to make it through each day. At home, a great part of my attention and energy is always spent calculating what my health can handle at the moment, or carefully budgeting and measuring out the day's activities in coffee spoons. I am sick, so I must follow through on healthcare tasks and appointments. I've had to do this in France, too, but much less, and I admit I feel as light as the air here.

Returning to this place has filled me up and replenished me – not only with the renewal of treasured friendships, with the sensual beauties of Paris, but also with the unforeseen joy of being able to walk around and go out more freely. These are the intoxications of ordinary life many of us take for granted. It has been ages since I've felt so restored. For 14 years now, I've been running on empty, so much has been taken from me. Not only the ability to travel and work but often even small aspects of life like being capable of making a quick trip to the grocery store, socializing with friends, or being able to digest a meal. Words cannot fully describe what it is like to be released back into the world after having been trapped in a life cut off from normalcy. This trip has given me a magnificent hope for the future and a dream that the shattered fragments of my life might yet come together.

☙

My mind wanders from Paris to Seattle. Memories of my fateful move float down now in tattered pieces, like leaves fallen from a shady grove into a stream. I see an overwhelming structure looming in front of me. It's the new office building I once excitedly readied myself to move into. It was a monument of industrial progress and would contain all the bustle of our business. There was palpable excitement over what a beautiful place it would be to work in, how efficient, how advanced. I feel anguish now when I think of how that building splintered my body, and with it, my entire life as well.

The only experience I could relate it to, which had imploded my life as severely, was the war I had lived through as a child in Egypt. Yet that event had not broken my world apart as completely, nor had it for nearly as long. I was only 10 years old, witnessing for the first time tragedy and the destruction people can wreak upon one another. I grew up a lot that year and would never be quite the same. I remember how I had returned from school one day to find our household in chaos and my frantic mother instructing my brother and me to quickly pack a suitcase with whatever we most valued, for we had to leave the country immediately. We must move now. We might never see our home again. I recall how we flew to Greece while my father stayed behind in Cairo, and how worried the rest of us were about his safety as well as that of our Egyptian friends, so much so that I had screaming nightmares for a long while and my mother and brother would break down and cry periodically throughout the day. Even though we eventually returned to Egypt, I would never see most of my school friends again. The move radically altered my life and my environment, and it taught me how daily life can erupt into violence and turmoil with the twinkle of one inauspicious star.

The memory of this other move, that concrete edifice, is strangely associated in my mind now with war because of the life-altering pain it brings as well – though this is a war that is somewhat more personal and is fought mostly inside of me, even though it deeply affected others, too.

This experience has the same feel of a life suddenly shattered and of the desperate need to rebuild it. First, I have had to tackle the foundation. For years, I have worked patiently to reconstruct my body. While it won't be the very same formation, I am now well enough for this trip to Paris. Here, aspects of French life have inspired me, and I've resolved to add them as building blocks to the newly fashioned life I hope to create. That's one of the things I have always loved about living abroad, cherry-picking elements of a culture that I enjoy and incorporating them into my life. Unexpectedly, this holiday has helped me feel as if I'm well on my way toward redesigning a completely new structure for my life.

A New Building

The day began in innocence. Outside the window, a faint rosy glow appeared on the horizon. From a newly built nest of twigs, a cheerful cathedral tune from the birds announced the new day and found its way to me. Inside, movers in brown uniforms circled around us like hounds fastened onto a promising scent. The office bustled with chatter, and the crackle of packing material mingled with the screech of furniture across the floor. Within our honeycombed cubicles, we piled boxes high with tools from our work life – books, computers and drafting lights. Once the boxes were filled, the movers eagerly scooped them up. With each packed box, the atmosphere grew livelier. Voices rose to a pitch as jokes sailed through the air. When a department director breezed through with a last-minute assignment for me, as if I had nothing else to do that day, my colleague Mike Harvey scuttled over and wisecracked, "Breathe slowly and count to 10!" His words would become prescient.

Amid this excitement, not a whisper of premonition hinted that with this move, my life would be pushed to the brink of cataclysmic change. It would be years before I would come to think of this ordinary day as the last day of life as I had known it. I thought to myself, I must remember to schedule a meeting with the caterer for the upcoming open house event so we can iron out the details while walking through the new building.

A mover interrupted my thoughts. "Is your computer ready to go?" he asked. I nodded. The telephone rang. I groped through the clutter, searching for the receiver. "Anne, about this upcoming event. ..." Laughing, I asked if it could wait until the following week. Trying to find my files in this chaos would be next to impossible. The rest of the world carried on with business as usual while our lives were put on slight hold. For those of us at the Puget Sound Trade District, our official business would be suspended until we reached the new offices, though the birds would carry on their own work.

☙

Eight years of my life had been spent in this building near the water's edge in Seattle, where I worked in the District's Communications Department. A publicly subsidized organization, the District was created to foster international trade and to stimulate the local economy. In Washington State, nearly one in every five jobs is linked to international trade. My particular work involved community relations and educating the public about the role trade played in our state. The job was a medley of tasks: planning international conferences and special events, finding speakers for community groups, and running an educational program for students from all over the county.

In that building, you could smell the salt water of Elliott Bay. You could hear the gulls' high-pitched cries. From my window, the Olympic Mountain range stretched across the horizon. To the south, beyond a thicket of orange shipping cranes, Mount Rainier hovered, colossal and surreal. On winter afternoons, I loved to watch the sun set, iridescent pink and gold hues bathing the Olympics' serrated peaks. It was equally exciting to see rainstorms moving in across the bay. On stormy days, boats bobbed on the choppy water, and birds flew backward above them. In the summer, barges piled high with motorboats, recreational vehicles, and pre-fabricated homes tied up to the piers, waiting for icy Alaskan waters to break up.

All 375 of us in the building eagerly anticipated the move. We were tired of the problems presented by an old building, especially the erratic heating and air-conditioning system that left staff on one end of the building sweltering while at the other end people shivered in sweaters. Our building manager inevitably answered our complaints by pointing at our open windows. "There's the problem," he would say. "The system can't work properly when you do that." Shaking his head, he would predict,

"You won't believe how much better it will be in the new building when you won't be able to open the windows." Complaints about the building to the Puget Sound Trade District's insurance manager got you nowhere either. He would inevitably throw up his hands and reply, "Wait until we get to heaven!" when staff approached him.

Our new office was supposed to be a little bit like heaven. Built down the street around the shell of an old fish cannery, the new building stretched longer than a football field, its facade punctuated by a rhythm of concrete columns. Broad entry steps led to an interior flooded with light, a dramatic two-story atrium that dominated the length of the building. A shallow stream carved in the slate floor quietly meandered through the airy space. Huge, exposed columns gave the interior a spare, industrial feeling. Everywhere, large windows offered sweeping views of a glittering Elliott Bay. Far in the distance, anchored ships were visible waiting to be unloaded, their decks stacked with metal containers.

One of the things I loved best about my work was not knowing exactly what each day would bring. But my favorite part was the people I worked with. Though there were inevitable tensions, the Communications Department was a group of fun, creative people who enjoyed working together, so much so that in our free time we periodically organized outings: biking in the San Juan Islands, cross-country skiing in the Cascade Mountains, or swimming parties on Hood Canal.

We had always worked hard while laughing our way through the day. Witty banter enlivened the atmosphere like balloons on a hot summer's day. Even on that moving day, amid the packing turmoil, the usual jokes and questions were served up as if we were in a short-order restaurant. Our comradeship came in handy because assignments often required all of us to work as a team. We took turns heading up projects. If an international conference was planned, for instance, I would manage the event, but all the other functions were delegated to the appropriate person. Our publications manager would create brochures and locate translators for them; our art director would design the printed materials; our media representative would handle publicity; our photographer would take pictures at the event and advise me about printing photographs for a conference directory; our staff assistants would help with everything and anything; and once the conference started, even our director and employee newsletter editor would spend time helping out at the hotel.

The first day in our new building everyone wandered around, faces beaming. After years in a crumbling, antiquated building we could hardly believe this would be our new home. What a move up. Walking down the hall, I passed Sharon Whiting, who worked in the Facilities Department, the group responsible for coordinating the construction. Usually she looked preoccupied and tired. That day she glowed like the pink orb of a setting sun.

"What a fine job your department has done, Sharon," I said. She smiled. "Not only is the building handsome, but you've completed it within budget."

"I'm glad you like it." Sharon tipped her head toward me and floated on down the hall as if drifting through her own dream.

Throughout the day, however, a strange lightheadedness began to plague me, along with ringing ears. Headache and nausea added to my symptoms by the afternoon. Things were piling up like bricks upon me. It was all very puzzling. I'd never felt this way before. I noticed the air in the building felt so stuffy and thick that you could almost cut through it. The offices smelled like a baked plastic bag and reeked of chlorine. At the end of the day, Joan Bell, the Communications Department publications manager, stopped by my office to ask how I felt. She told me she'd had a bad headache and ringing ears all day. Other staff members were feeling unwell too. Joan wondered if it was related to the noxious odors permeating the building. She grimaced when I told her I'd been feeling nauseous and lightheaded as well.

Some of the fumes came from artists and construction workers who were still finishing up their work throughout the building. Outside our department, an artist was painting a decorative wall. Another was applying mosaic tile to a concrete column downstairs, and the odor of glue was wafting up to our area. Other men wearing facemasks were putting final touches on the wood paneling. In our department, the plastic-smelling odor seemed stronger, and the air stuffier, than in other parts of the building. Joan and I went to George Patrello, the District's industrial hygienist, with our questions.

"This weekend the building will be flushed with outside air to help push out the chemical fumes," he explained. "Next, the ventilation system will be balanced to ensure the air is moving evenly throughout the building." George paused. "Usually this is done before employees occupy new offices, but the District is behind schedule and they needed to stick to the move-in date."

Once I got home, my symptoms disappeared. That night I slept soundly, tired after a busy day. But when I returned to the building the next day, the symptoms came back. Each day they got progressively worse, like radio static getting louder and louder, and each day when I left work they disappeared. After several weeks, the nearly constant headaches escalated to feeling like a meat cleaver banging against my brain. The nausea had intensified, forcing me to swallow throughout the day to keep from throwing up. Relentless ear ringing and dizziness made me unsteady on my feet. I couldn't think clearly. My head was groggy and thick as soup. When someone asked me a question, I felt tongue-tied and struggled to summon up simple words to answer. Toughest on me was having symptoms that were largely invisible to others. If you looked closely, my eyes did appear strained, my manner tired. But most of the time I looked fine.

Even visitors volunteered that they were plagued by headaches and nausea while attending meetings in our building, though some were there as little as an hour. Their problems went away as soon as they left. But no one would report symptoms for fear of losing District business. A few visitors also remarked that some parts of the building seemed worse than others. Smells, they noticed, were stronger in our end of the building, where ceilings were lower. I noticed I breathed more easily inside the directors' offices. Could larger offices have better air, I wondered?

The third week after our move into the new office, things changed. My symptoms no longer disappeared within hours of leaving the building. It now took two days outside the office before they would go away. Sunday nights I would begin to feel better, only to have the problems resume Monday morning. This isn't a good direction, I'd think, wondering what to do.

The timing couldn't have been worse. To celebrate the grand opening of our building, our Communications Department was planning a series of events for Puget Sound Trade District customers, employees and their families, and the community. Planning for the opening events was so demanding that I forced myself to carry on, hoping my troubles would fade away. I received permission from my director, Marian Dixon, to work at home in the afternoons until the parties were over; meetings were now scheduled for the mornings and my concentrated work was left for the afternoons. Mercifully, about an hour after leaving the building, the fog in my head would clear enough for me to focus.

Still, according to e-mails sent to Joan and me, the building hadn't been flushed with outside air and the ventilation system hadn't been balanced. Each week there were promises from the Employee Health and Safety Department that it would be done the following weekend, and each Monday they'd cite another reason for why it hadn't happened. In any case, with thousands of visitors about to descend on the site, I continued to try to push the symptoms from my mind. There would be time to see my doctor when everything settled down. In the meantime, I simply hoped the problem would go away.

༄

Those early days were carefree ones. I knew nothing then about sick-building syndrome, a term referring to health problems suffered by workers in modern office buildings. Building-related illnesses were prevalent enough, however, that the World Health Organization estimated one in three employees might be working in a place that was making them sick. Health symptoms varied from person to person, but they most commonly included headaches, nausea, dizziness, short-term memory loss, irritability, itchy eyes and throats, asthma, and possible damage to the nervous and respiratory systems.

The problem remains little understood largely because there is no single culprit. A dizzying array of chemicals and contaminants can hang in a workplace's air. What is known is that since the advent of energy-efficient construction in the 1970s, sick-building syndrome has been on the rise. Cases have increased more than 40 percent. Some think

17

the health problem has reached almost epidemic proportions. There are no specific tests a doctor can run to determine whether a patient's symptoms have been triggered by a sick building. Instead, the health problem is a diagnosis of exclusion, meaning doctors issue an opinion after eliminating all other possible causes of the symptoms.

Sick-building syndrome emerged in the 1970s and its cause remains elusive, although two general changes in society in recent decades have been widely suspected. First, because of the energy crisis in 1973-74, building construction practices changed considerably. To cut energy costs, architects began to design buildings tightly sealed with thick layers of insulation so air couldn't enter or escape, and with windows that no longer opened. The ventilation system then became the mechanical lungs of the building and office air quality depended entirely on it. To save money, building operators recirculated much of the indoor air and reduced the amount of fresh air brought in. Staff at the Occupational Safety & Health Administration (OSHA), who have investigated more than 1,000 sick buildings, say the problem typically is caused by multiple reasons, but one of them usually involves an inadequate ventilation system. When experts investigate a building's air quality, they usually have more success gathering information through low-tech methods – for instance, interviewing employees and custodians or doing a "walk-through" of the building – instead of sophisticated techniques used by industrial hygienists.

The second simultaneous trend that might have contributed toward sick-building syndrome is that the numbers of chemicals used inside office buildings and in constructing them has exploded. From 1970 to 1990, the use of chemicals in the production of building materials and furnishings increased more than fivefold. Add to that the increased use of fume-producing machines such as computer printers and fax machines, together with the residue from cleaning products and pesticides, and you have a chemical soup sloshing around in these hermetically sealed buildings.

Whatever the specific causes of sick-building syndrome, poor indoor air ranks as one of the top five environmental health risks of our time, according to the U.S. Environmental Protection Agency. Indoor air may be two to five times more polluted than outdoor air, and in the beginning months of a new building, it can be 100 times worse. Despite the fact that we spend 90 percent of our time inside, with more than half of that at work, the federal government doesn't have effective standards for indoor air quality in offices. OSHA has set standards to protect workers against individual contaminants, such as benzene and formaldehyde, but they were meant for industrial workplaces, not white-collar offices. Besides, workers are getting sick despite those standards. Moreover, the standards don't address the combined effect of breathing in multiple chemicals at once because scientists don't yet know for certain how to measure for these combinations. Chemicals might act synergistically, becoming more dangerous together than each of them is on its own — the way alcohol taken with certain medications can amplify a drug's effects.

Research indicates poor indoor air quality takes a financial toll on the workplace. One study showed that reduced productivity, due to sick-building syndrome, of just five or 10 minutes per day would cost an employer from $636 to $2,444 per affected employee per year, depending on his or her salary. A Danish study found that typists increased their output by six percent in offices with cleaner air. Research has also indicated the financial benefits of improving indoor office climates can be eight to 17 times greater than the costs of making those improvements.

In a sense, sick-building syndrome illnesses may bear similarities to other health problems that are suspected to be linked, at least partly, to air pollution. The rate of asthma has doubled since 1980, and allergies have been on the rise since the 1970s. No one knows for sure why this is happening, but many experts think air pollution may be partly to blame. Studies show the more polluted a city, the higher its residents' rate of heart disease. A white man of the baby boom generation is twice as likely to develop cancer as his grandfather, a statistic many think may be due to cancer-causing chemicals in the environment. Our chemical culture has been suspected to be associated even with health problems that aren't specific illnesses, such as the tripling of the infertility rate since World War II. According to one study, sperm counts among American men have dropped 50 percent in the last 50 years. Again, no one can yet be certain about why, but we do know some chemicals can destroy a man's reproductive system. For example, numerous male workers were sterilized by daily exposure to dibromochloropropane (DBCP), a pesticide they were manufacturing at a California plant in 1977.

I would not learn about any of this for another year. First I would have to stumble from one healthcare provider to the next before finally finding people with some knowledge of the problem, although no one could be an expert on the topic. Meanwhile, I cast about in the dark, fumbling for light. Slowly, a rough outline of the illness began to form.

Before my chemical-related illness, I tended to believe diseases and other major sicknesses practically sprang up overnight. I would hear of a friend who had just learned he had cancer, and I would feel incredulous because he had seemed to be in perfect health only the week before. But exposures to daily chemicals may quietly and slowly build up in our bodies over many years, without obvious warning signs. After all, we eat chemicals in food, we breathe them in, and toxic gasses and liquids can easily be absorbed through our porous skin and quickly find their way into our bloodstream. It may be that our bodies fill up silently like sponges for many years until something just gives. I don't know, but I hope someday we will understand it.

Set Adrift on Wild Seas

We were curled up on the sofa in our lemon-yellow living room, clinging to one another as if on a shipwrecked raft, hopeful that if we held each other tightly enough we might keep our mounting problems from capsizing us. Ted held me as I cried softly, listening to the litany of my frustrations. One month after moving to the new building, I could barely get through the workday. At home, all I could muster was the energy to stagger to the couch and collapse in a heap until bedtime. I pressed myself into Ted's neck, finding comfort in the rise and fall of his breath, in his earthy scent.

"Anne," he whispered, "I'm growing alarmed at how quickly your health is deteriorating." Deep furrows spread across his forehead more regularly these days.

A tall, slim, dark-haired man, Ted possessed infinite patience and a great sense of humor, which would hold up well and buoy us in the years to come. Often he would sit back and take it all in, and then comment on what he noticed in an amusing way. Ted's take on my fabric purchases was typical. In those days, I sewed most of my clothes and even found time to make Ted some custom-fitted shirts. There wasn't a fabric sale I could pass up. Coming home with yet more material, I would find Ted grinning and calling me a *fabric-holic*.

"With all the material you buy, we may end up in the poorhouse. But at least we'll be the best-dressed people there!" He would chuckle. I would choke with laughter.

I loved the romantic streak in Ted. Many times I'd stumbled across a note or gift he had tucked into my purse or cereal bowl. In advance of my birthday, he once went to a restaurant ahead of time to arrange a special menu for the event. When we arrived, the dishes flowed seamlessly out of the kitchen: king salmon encased in puff pastry, escargot, a bottle of their finest champagne. Afterward we went dancing, a favorite pastime of ours. The 12 years we had been together had been exceedingly happy ones. I didn't think it was possible for a couple to be happier. But on this particular evening, neither of us found any humor in my growing health troubles.

"Are you ready to hear about the latest episode of 'As the District Turns?'" I asked him, a grim smile at the corners of my mouth. Ted sighed, knowing my District stories could go on and on.

I told him I was beginning to feel bad that my health problems were creating more work for others: "Today a staff assistant had to spend quite some time looking for files for me because I'm only in the building in the mornings."

"Anne, would you snap out of it?" Ted exclaimed, his brown eyes blazing like a three-alarm fire. He pulled me closer. "It's the District management that should feel bad. I just wish there were something I could do to help. I feel so helpless watching your health plummet."

Ted looked into my eyes, drinking them in, trying to understand the person I was becoming since illness had struck. In truth I couldn't even explain myself to him, so confused had my life become, especially in that moment. There was much I didn't understand then, much I still had to learn. I only knew that with our move into the new office building, my life had tumbled off a cliff, and I despaired about trying to pick up the shattered pieces. I closed my eyes, nestled against Ted's shoulder, and shuddered at how quickly life can force change on you. One day I had been healthy, able to work a full day with ease and go out with Ted or friends at night. Now all I wanted to do was lie on the sofa.

❧

I found I wasn't the only one with aggravated health issues. Joan Bell's symptoms were also growing worse. A 15-year veteran of the District, she was usually a calm person who balanced work and family life with the finesse of an air traffic controller. Meet deadlines. Attend meetings. Lead staff. Create publications. Drive the children to school and baseball practice. Supervise homework. A fine-boned brunette with short, wavy hair, Joan had a self-deprecating sense of humor and philosophical views of life that helped her manage it all. She had a knack for taking care of family priorities while letting go of unimportant details. Weeds could proliferate in her yard, her house could look lived-in, but the important things got done.

Joan often poked fun at her sensible skirts and tailored jackets. "I really have excellent taste," she would tell people, "but you wouldn't know it by looking at me!" When she worked with an especially difficult person, Joan, a devout Catholic, would say under her breath, "I hope every hour I spend working with Peter is going to be an hour knocked off my stay in purgatory."

Within weeks of moving to the new building, this energetic woman went from being the paragon of responsibility to missing long stretches of work. She had seldom taken sick days before. Now Joan dragged herself around, agitated and fatigued. She couldn't sleep at night because her ears rang so loudly. Exasperated, she sent an e-mail message to our department's office manager. The potent and noxious odor in our building was intolerable, Joan complained. She was suffering from persistent headaches and nosebleeds. The District, rather than expecting her to take pain medication every four hours, should address the root of the problem.

The industrial hygienist grew increasingly distant from Joan and me. Normally a conscientious, responsive person, George, it seemed, wanted to help but didn't have enough authority to do so. George's promises to flush the building had mysteriously changed to helpful replies like, "I'll pass your comments on to the safety committee."

"This is bureaucracy at its best!" I joked to Joan in an exasperated moment. She shook her head.

One day I was talking to George. "We've been in this building a month," I said, "and it's frightening how quickly my health is deteriorating."

"Anne," George replied, "I'm sorry but I have to wash my hands of the situation."

I was stunned, as if he'd just run over me with his car. How could he leave me dangling like that, I wondered. Problems like mine were part of his job responsibilities. Soon afterward, the Health and Safety Department was directed not to handle air quality complaints. From then on, the Facilities Department would be responsible for them.

Reading between the lines, the employees got the message. The task had been shifted away from the department charged with employee health to the one responsible for taking care of the building. In case we had doubts about the District's priorities, they were cleared up by an e-mail from one of the senior directors, who explained why the ventilation system still hadn't been balanced to make sure air flowed evenly throughout the building. This time the delay was attributed to the need to protect office equipment.

Losing patience, I raised the air quality issue in our department's weekly staff meeting. I told my director I'd like to discuss the health symptoms some of us had been experiencing since moving to the building. I recounted how Joan and I had been trying to get help from George, but he'd been directed not to get involved and said Facilities had taken over the matter. Everyone's heads swiveled toward me.

"How many people aren't feeling well today – from what they think are problems related to the building?" director Marian asked. Five of the 12 of us raised our hands. "Molly, why don't you send an e-mail to Facilities to inform them of our situation," Marian continued.

After the meeting, assistant Molly sent a message to Facilities saying five members of our department were feeling ill. All of them, she pointed out, sat in cubicle offices with higher walls, and she wondered if this might be a clue to the illnesses. Sharon Whiting from the Facilities Department responded by suggesting that our health symptoms might be due to other causes.

If Joan and I had been looking for a touch of drama, Sharon's unexpected visit to our department wouldn't have disappointed us. In she strode one day like a general ready to put down insubordinate troops. Hands on her hips, glancing around our offices, she seemed to be looking for a visible cause of all the health complaints.

"Your problems must be from the stress of these stupid events! Joan, have you had your blood pressure checked? Once I had headaches and ear ringing myself. My doctor told me I had such high blood pressure, I was on the verge of having a stroke!" She paused, built up more steam, then added, "This is not a sick building!" and stomped off.

A sick building? I thought. How in the world could a building be sick? What did I have to do to be taken seriously around here?

According to colleagues, Sharon had begun referring to Joan and me as hypochondriacs and troublemakers. I was grieved to see the good relationship I'd had with Sharon and the Facilities Department deteriorate so quickly. Over the years, I had worked on several projects for Facilities. The staff there had been a pleasure to work with and they liked my results. Sharon was the same person who had once told my boss she valued my instincts so highly that I could propose new ideas and she would try them, simply because of my track record. But now that my instincts and physical symptoms warned of air quality problems, this was a different story.

Admittedly, the Facilities staff was under enormous pressure. Long months of completing the building had taken their toll. Adding to the strain, the department's reputation was at stake. They were particularly worried the public might criticize them for spending too much money. Building the new Puget Sound Trade District offices was less expensive than renovating the old fish processing plant and moving our staff to temporary quarters. Still, some complained it was an extravagant move. Others praised the district for urban renewal, hailing the new office as one of the most beautiful public buildings Seattle had seen go up in a long time.

The Facilities department had gone to great lengths to create a polished-looking building. Sometimes this was taken to an extreme: Staff could have only District-supplied plants in their offices; employees were encouraged to use the white coffee mugs in the kitchens rather than their own motley assortment; and people couldn't have fans in their offices. Mine was confiscated after I had put it there to improve my cubicle's stagnant air.

One of the members of the District's board of directors told a friend of mine that employees only imagined their illnesses, saying it was "all in their heads." Given the lack of response from higher-ups, Joan and I became unwitting magnets for employee complaints. Some colleagues told us about headaches, and others had flu-like symptoms, sinus problems, nausea or vomiting. Many found breathing difficult while in the building. Some staff with pre-existing health problems found that their conditions had worsened in the new building. Employees weren't getting any assistance from their doctors, many of whom were simply diagnosing stress. The doctors had little to go on, not being able to evaluate all affected employees.

Our department, once so high-spirited, had lost its fun-loving edge. A somber mood had invaded our group like a virus. Where once we had gone to work and laughed our way through the day, now staff in our department clustered together to tally up health symptoms in low, discouraged voices. One month into the new building, employees throughout the District were making an effort to keep up with Joan's and my efforts to resolve the situation. Many who weren't speaking out of fear of being labeled troublemakers hoped our outspokenness would generate solutions for the whole building.

It seemed to reassure staff to know that others had similar symptoms. Some admitted they would rather risk their health than their job security. Others reported having supervisors who punished employees for bringing forward bad news. My department seemed to tolerate free speech more than most. Later on, when I talked to employees in other sick buildings, I learned this fear of retaliation was typical. Most workers, it turned out, were afraid of losing their jobs or of having their work environment grow intolerable because of their health troubles. A few workers reported that their employers were open and responsive, but those were a minority.

One day a telephone call from a coworker, Gary Fowler, left me particularly disturbed. After discussing a mutual work project, he asked me about my health symptoms, showing unusual interest. Suddenly his voice dropped. I strained to hear him. "I'm having health problems, too," he whispered, "but I've been threatened to keep quiet. The stories I could tell you...but I'm not at my desk right now." His voice trailed off, then he hung up. With all the uninvited reports, I was beginning to feel like a private detective who hadn't applied for the job.

Unsolicited reports from other employees continued. A staff person in the District's Industrial Hygiene Department told me he had approached Sharon in the Facilities Department when the building was in the design stage to discuss improving indoor air quality. Apparently she brushed him off. Another person called me to say construction workers had experienced unusually severe levels of health problems while working on the building.

Joan and I quickly tired of being unofficial ombudsmen for health complaints, especially as there was nothing more we could do about them. I had asked the managers to designate a contact person for sick employees. I may as well have been speaking Hindi for all the good it did. The reluctance to appoint a contact person conveyed a strong message: avoiding liability and keeping costs down would take precedence over employee health – because, I assumed, recognizing the problem might have involved spending money on improved ventilation or on compensating sick employees. The District may also have feared lawsuits; ironically, if they found evidence of something that might sicken employees, that might strengthen an employee's case against the District. No one seemed to question how much money might be lost owing to increased absenteeism and reduced productivity.

Overall, the District had been a good, progressive employer, and I had found it a satisfying place to work. But with the reports continuing to roll in, I was beginning to question this track record. Harriet Bly, in the Personnel Department, called to say she was in a conference where a man introduced himself as the contractor hired to install the District's ventilation system. This man claimed he had recommended a ventilation system that cost more than Facilities had budgeted. When he protested that a cheaper system would be inadequate, Sharon Whiting allegedly had him removed from the project. Apparently the building permit application process only required the District to show that its planned system met certain ventilation levels; once the building was up and operating, the District didn't have to prove it functioned as designed.

☙

I'll never forget the day of the opening ceremony, five weeks after we moved into the new building. The setting was magnificent. Behind the podium, a lavender-blue painted wall framed the misty silhouette of the Olympic Mountains and the shimmering navy water of Elliott Bay. Government trade officials from Ireland gave speeches in charming lilting accents. One of them even sang a song. The District president thanked the Facilities Department for its hard work, and one of the board of directors talked about the importance of staying competitive in international trade. All the while, I was watching from the audience, barely able to stand up, much less concentrate. It took an enormous effort to talk to colleagues next to me. Simply clapping in applause only made me dizzier and more nauseous. That night, despairing, I wondered what to do. I came to the conclusion that the special events would be over shortly – then I could figure out how to respond.

As it turned out, my body couldn't wait. The morning of our reception for 600 customers, I struggled to rise at the crack of dawn. My head spun like a whirling dervish, and standing up only made it worse. Somehow I pulled on a rustling green silk dress and staggered out the door, hoping that setting myself in motion might alleviate my dizziness. Arriving at work barely functioning, I lay down in the employee lounge, desperately willing the symptoms to subside enough for me to get through the day. The walls of the darkened lounge seemed to throb in frenetic gasps, and the couch beneath me seemed to bob about on a stormy sea. An hour later, my symptoms had not improved. It was clear I'd have to see my doctor. Back at my desk, I dialed her office, while colleagues passed by, asking me how the reception was going. "I'm feeling awful," I kept saying. "Could we talk later?"

After scheduling an appointment, I called industrial hygienist George. He suggested reporting my troubles to the Workers' Compensation Department. Although I had vaguely known of this program, I'd assumed it was for employees with physically active or dangerous jobs – not office work like mine. I figured it wouldn't hurt to file an injury report.

After filling out the forms in the Workers' Compensation Department, I drove to my doctor's office and missed the reception. It occurred to me that taking a taxi would have been smarter. My muscles twitched, my discombobulated mind struggled to focus, my head felt as if a boulder was crushing it. I didn't know if I could make it to the doctor's. There, while checking in with the receptionist, I began throwing up. Miserable as things were, at last there was visible proof of illness! I felt relieved. And my doctor believed me.

A ginger-haired woman with a passion for music, Dr. Carol Osborne had been my primary care physician for more than 10 years. She said she thought I was suffering from fumes and poor ventilation. She recommended I stay home, avoiding fumes for two weeks, and said this might alleviate my symptoms. She filled out a form to have my blood checked for carbon monoxide poisoning. In the meantime, she told me to get the District to improve its ventilation. I told her I had been trying to do just that.

"You may be the District's canary in the mine shaft, so they should care," Dr. Osborne said emphatically. "You might be only the first one to get so sick, but the building might be polluting other people's systems as well."

Days passed by in a blur. All food and water came right back up. The slightest movement triggered waves of nausea. My insides quivered and lurched like a train thrown off a railroad track. My daily life, it seemed, had become a kind of tragic-comic farce. Getting into bed took several hours. Ted was out of town. I stumbled up the stairs, my head feeling swollen, nausea rising with every step. I crawled into bed to avoid another vomiting jag; it was difficult to stop once I began. Lying on my left side with an arm resting over my ears helped relieve the drilling head pain a bit. My ears rang with a windy, whistling tunnel sound.

I fumbled with my zipper, trying to get my jeans off without worsening the nausea. Mission accomplished: pants off. Another 20-minute break to rest up for the next stage. Now the shirt. This was no small task, as it involved sitting up. I quickly pulled the shirt over my head and lay down.

The telephone on my bedside table rang. Answer it and risk triggering more nausea? Or let the answering machine get it? I picked it up feeling terribly alone, needing to hear someone's voice. It was my friend Karen. Guessing from my garbled, weak voice that something was amiss, she asked me what was wrong. But talking only made the nausea swell. Suddenly I felt like I was on that seasick ship again, tossing and pitching to and fro, and I had to bail out. I'll call you back, I said, sadly dropping the receiver to the outside world.

Lifting the Fabric of Life

Days passed like crashing waves. My symptoms subsided enough that I could begin working on the last special event from home, on an open house for the public. During those two weeks, District colleagues called with the latest news from the front. Battles about the building and illnesses were raging by e-mail. One message from our Communications office manager to Facilities asked why the District wasn't more aggressive in the removal of the screens over the air vents because we were told our air circulation would be much improved if they were removed. We were made to understand the idea was rejected since doing so would not fit in with the architectural design.

Another message from the Communications Department asked Facilities if our troubles might be related to the strong chlorine odors. Visitors had mentioned that our end of the building smelled like a swimming pool. Facilities staff answered each e-mail with reasons why they did not plan to take any action.

Articles began appearing in local newspapers. A few people in the new District building had developed sick-building syndrome, the *Seattle Times* reported. The newspaper article mentioned that the District had hired an environmental and engineering expert to test the air. This was the first I had heard of tests being ordered. A District spokesperson was quoted downplaying the situation by saying employee complaints had "subsided."

During the weeks at home, my symptoms gradually disappeared. Finally I returned to work, certain my problem was cured since I now felt back to my old self. The first day back was quiet and uneventful. With opening events behind me, I spent the day setting up my new office. That night, however, waves of nausea, ringing ears and splitting head pain woke me up like a bolt of lightning. I lay in bed, despair engulfing me like a thick, ominous fog. This can't be happening, I thought. Please, oh please, let it be a bad dream. I tossed and turned until a rosy glow appeared on the horizon. It was time to get up and try another day in the office.

To my great horror, that day my symptoms only grew worse. I began reacting to virtually any chemical I was exposed to at home and at the office. Things that had never bothered me before now had sickening aromas. Dry-cleaning fluids, auto exhaust, new clothes, the grocery store – all set off my symptoms. An overpowering stench wafted up from the highway when I drove down the ramp. I would change lanes if an old car got in front of me because its exhaust smelled worse than newer, less polluting cars. When I walked into friends' homes where they cooked on gas stoves, I could smell gas in the air. Even though I'd always enjoyed perfume, now people wearing fragrances emitted nauseating odors like skunks.

Another year would pass before I would learn the name for what was happening: multiple chemical sensitivity. The condition involves greatly increased sensitivity to a wide range of synthetic chemicals. It can come on suddenly – for example, when someone moves to a new office building or is exposed to pesticides. Or the illness can develop gradually over a lifetime of repeated exposures to low levels of toxins. Once a person is sensitized, even a whiff of perfume can trigger a cascade of symptoms. Recent studies have indicated 15 percent of the population may suffer from chemical sensitivities, mainly due to poor indoor air quality and the growing prevalence of chemicals in our air, food and products – although not all in that 15 percent are as hypersensitive to chemicals as I have become.

Many years later, I became astounded by how many people in the general population react to everyday chemicals, not just those of us with multiple chemical sensitivity or those who work in energy-efficient office buildings. But such affected people probably will never have their health problems completely diagnosed. In a way, I was fortunate to have my illness begin suddenly that first day in the building because it made obvious the source of my symptoms.

The particular strain of my chemical-related illness and similar ailments of the population at large don't fit the medical community's understanding of disease, so mainstream physicians don't know how to explain or treat the illnesses. People with MCS, for example, are reacting to chemicals at lower levels than have been thought to cause harm. Nor does the condition fit a true allergy because physicians can't measure it by the usual methods of testing for allergies. Nevertheless, like sick-building syndrome, the problem appears to be growing. In its worst form, MCS can be debilitating, forcing a person to stay at home, unable to even have guests over unless they refrain from using perfume or fragranced laundry products. Just because chemical effects on health can be subtle, that does not mean they are not powerful in their own way.

But at this point, I didn't realize how severe the health problem could get. All I could cling to was a flickering hope that things would return to normal. Just seeing neighbors leave for work in the morning made me jealous. The simple rituals of daily life were suddenly beyond reach. For me, it was an accomplishment just to make it through the day. Each moment took great effort. The telephone's ring irritated me. Talking with other people required concentration just to understand what they were saying. I started to wonder how long life could go on like this. And whenever I thought surely things couldn't get worse, somehow they did.

To say my wings had been clipped would have been an understatement. Now, merely running an errand was a big trip. Each venture out had to be scrupulously planned so I would avoid chemicals that might trigger symptoms. Places like department stores presented particular challenges because clothing was permeated with formaldehyde and other chemicals used in fabrics. Having to go to extreme lengths to do something as simple as buying a shirt made me feel like a pariah and a freak. Life had indeed become surreal.

Being housebound was a drastic change – an ironic turn of events for someone who loved travel and adventure as much as I did. One night Ted tossed several maps on the bed with hopes of cheering me up. Ted was just as passionate about traveling as I was. Most years found us vacationing abroad, happily exploring little-traveled country roads or drinking in art museums.

"How about planning our next trip?" Ted asked, his eyes bright and shining, as if his enthusiasm might become infectious.

"Oh, Ted," I said, sinking down under the covers, "I can't think about that right now."

He looked at me with dismay. Things were not usually this way. An evening spent poring over maps would usually transport me with wild hopes and visions of things beyond my little corner of the world.

∽

Having been born to adventurous parents, I had lived a peripatetic childhood. My parents took me abroad at the age of one to live in Accra, Ghana, a rectangular-shaped African country between Nigeria and the Ivory Coast, on the Gulf of Guinea. Ghana had just won her independence from the British, the first black African country to do so. There, my father helped set up and teach at the first black-African business school in Africa and we lived in a neighborhood where people sat at the dinner table with tennis rackets to keep the bats out of the food. Eight months after we arrived in Ghana, my brother was born, delivered by an African midwife.

In those days Accra was a major port city. My brother and I especially loved going down to the beach and watching ships as they were loaded. We were mesmerized by the crews of men, singing in unison, running through the rough surf with bags of cocoa on their backs as they deposited their cargo into small boats and rowed back out to anchored ships. Back then I was a healthy child, not given to spending much time indoors, especially since the climate was so warm.

Just before I started first grade, we moved to Egypt. Our home, just outside Cairo, was an art deco stucco villa built with rounded walls, like a steamer setting out to sea, with a necklace of orchid trees planted around the property. The Holy Family was said to have stayed at the Coptic monastery near our home on the banks of the Nile River. From the monastery, as the story goes, they embarked for Upper Egypt. My father would make the daily drive from our villa into Cairo, where he had a position with the Ford Foundation. The foundation gave out grants to establish projects like a national family planning program and an institute to reclaim desert land for agriculture.

My classmates came from 27 different countries throughout the world. At the time, this hardly seemed unusual, because at my preschool in Ghana I had been one of the few white children in my class. But the view from my new school delighted me. Camels with gangly legs and splendid long-tooting grunts lumbered about a dirt courtyard across the street, their heads bobbing back and forth at the end of tall, curved necks. They formed the police department's desert patrol division. Camels are more effective for prowling the desert than cars for they don't get stuck in the sand and can go for days without water. At Christmastime, our school would rent three of the camels for our nativity pageant and the wise men would ride them onto the stage. Sometimes goats and *gamoosas*, black water buffalo crowned with curved horns, also sauntered down the street, prodded on by their owner.

By our second year in Egypt, I had two younger brothers. To escape the summer heat during those years, my parents took us traveling throughout Europe and America. For several summers, we rented a chalet in the Austrian Alps or we visited relatives back home in South Carolina and New Jersey. Travel was in our blood – so much so that for periods of time after my family returned to the United States, I chose to live with families in India and France. Some of my friends' parents were aghast that my mother and father would let their 17-year-old daughter go to India. My parents' attitude was, Isn't it great? None of us has ever been there! Given all the germs and viruses I was exposed to as a child, it later struck me as ironic that a modern American office building would disable my health. Much later, some District staff members and friends would wonder if growing up in Africa could have caused my chemical illness. The new office sickened at least 60 District staffers and even some visitors, I'd reply, and none of them grew up in Africa.

My adventurous spirit later took me to Seattle after I graduated from Princeton University. Single and jobless, I had never been to the Northwest, nor did any friends await me there. This was one undertaking my parents did not enthusiastically support. They sensibly entreated me, "Why don't you move to a city where we know people who can help you find a job and get settled?" But my mind was made up. Years later, I felt that moving to Seattle had been one of the best decisions of my life.

❧

Ted interrupted my thoughts. "We can at least think about a trip, can't we? Nothing has to be definite." I propped myself up on one elbow, trying to humor him.

"I'm thinking of a trip like the one we made to Egypt," I said, "because it was so exotic." We began to reminisce.

A sweltering 108-degree day had greeted us when we arrived in Cairo in late June, a heat wave even by Egyptian standards. Mirages shimmered above the tarmac, and the asphalt felt like marshmallow under my feet. The air blazed hot, so hot that I gasped upon emerging from the airplane. Mr. and Mrs. Madkour, longtime Egyptian family friends, waved at us through the window as we waited to clear Customs. "Achlan-wu-sah-lan," they called out, their words rumbling up from the back of their throats. "It's so good to see you!" Part of me felt I had come home.

We remembered our morning at the Cairo Museum fondly. A symphony of blaring horns filled the air as Mrs. Madkour drove us to Tahrir Square in her white Fiat, cars weaving in and out ahead of us as if the lanes were irrelevant. Along the way, a tangle of streets pulsed with cars and buses, with donkeys and camels moving in every conceivable direction. Pedestrians threaded their way through the mayhem as if surfing a crest of powerful waves. A car blocking a lane posed no impediment. Drivers simply veered over onto the sidewalk, even turned the wrong way up a one-way street, to get around it. My heart leapt to my throat more than once as we zoomed this way and that, heading in the general direction of the museum. Peering over my shoulder, I could see Ted clutching his seatbelt, then grasping the edge of his seat when we screeched to an abrupt halt. We had made a pact, Ted and I, that the two of us would take turns sitting in the front seat where we had a head-on view of the near-misses and collisions, because being there could feel terrifying. I looked over at Mrs. Madkour, her body relaxed like rubber,

36

as she smiled and chatted on to us, oblivious to the chaos. Finally we spotted a parking place.

A slim man in a collarless shirt and long khaki pants waved his arms, beckoning us into the spot. He was part of a population of men called car-parks who eked out their living by appointing themselves guardians of cars parked along the street. We gave him a baksheesh, or tip. The car park might roll down our windows upon our return, maybe wipe the windshield with his dirty rag. My father used to jokingly refer to this tipping custom as a share-the-wealth program.

Beyond a ring of palm trees lay the imposing sand-colored museum painted with a light powdering of dust. As we walked up the broad entrance steps, the smell of garlic wafted over from the corner felafel stand. Our tour guide, Nadia Assaad, first took us to the second floor because Mrs. Madkour had arranged for us to see the mummy of Pharoah Ramses II. Light had deteriorated his body so much that he lay hidden in a glass case draped with a maroon velvet cloth. The year before the museum had sent the damaged mummy to Paris for restoration work. My sister-in-law Judy, who lived in Paris, had laughed when she told us how Ramses' mummy was driven down the Champs-Élysées in a motorcade, as any visiting dignitary would be.

Nadia lifted the fabric. We stood back, breathless at the sight of the 3,000-year-old mummy. Before us was the only pharaoh to convince people he was a god while he was living. We had just seen numerous colossal-sized statues of him in upper Egypt – four 65-foot statues of him adorned the entrance to the Temple of Abu Simbel alone. I had trembled with awe when I had stood before the temple, especially at how I only came up to the ankle of one of those statues.

"Anne, can you believe how well-preserved his features are?" Ted had asked, pulling me toward the slight body with nut-brown skin, his ancient balding head fringed with white wispy hair. The sight of the pharaoh triggered a flood of memories from my childhood – of one school vacation spent touring the pharaohs' tombs, of my brother and me slithering along the sands of the Sahara Desert as we dug up mummy beads and other ancient artifacts, of camping in the desert beneath a canopy of glittering stars hung from a velvet sky. Ted interrupted my far-off musings and led me over to the display of King Tut's treasures.

⁙

During my follow-up appointment with Dr. Osborne, when I described my escalating problems, she suggested I get another job because things weren't looking good. She told me I had become hypersensitive to chemical fumes. This sounded drastic to me. After all, I liked my job. And how could I look for another job in my condition? How did I know another office wouldn't exacerbate my symptoms? Dr. Osborne then said if not another job, maybe I should seek a three-month leave of absence.

In accordance with Dr. Osborne's recommendation, the District allowed me to work from home for three months. Meanwhile, reports from other employees about building-related health problems didn't let up. When my office was loaned to an employee from another department, she began to feel ill the first day. Curiously, she hadn't had problems while working in other departments. An employee sent an e-mail to Facilities reporting her nausea. Another, after moving to our department, began missing days of work. She had felt better working elsewhere in the building. The situation was like playing musical chairs, I told Joan one day, because at the end of the day you didn't know who would be left standing. Joan still suffered from headaches and ear ringing, but her symptoms had stabilized enough so she could carry on. Then there was Helen Smith in the Equal Employment Opportunity Department. At first Helen thought she had the flu. Her head grew congested the first day in the new building. Burning eyes followed. She grew suspicious when she lost her voice and felt as if her throat were closing. So Helen stayed home for a few days and her symptoms improved. But as soon as she returned to the office, her problems came back.

Helen was puzzled by her reactions because she had been in the office often while it was being built, to make sure contractors were complying with regulations. But at the time, she would be there for only one hour, and the building had not yet been sealed. Helen's doctors seemed at a loss to diagnose her health troubles. At first her physicians thought that she had the flu; then they told her she had a sinus infection; later they

38

blamed it on allergies. I keep going to the doctors, Helen said, but they just keep naming my symptoms something else.

A manager in the Marketing Department who had worked at the District for 13 years also suffered from building-related symptoms. Before moving to the new office, he did not have any health problems. But shortly thereafter, he experienced nosebleeds, just as Joan had. It alarmed him a bit, but he soon forgot about it when the bleeding went away. Next, however, he found himself short of breath when inside the building, and this time the problem persisted.

Several months after the District's move into new offices, I knew of 60 people, out of 375 staffers, who believed they were suffering from office-related health problems. And I didn't know every person in the building. Yet the myth persisted – in officialdom anyway – that Joan and I were the only sick employees. Only staff members who filed injury reports were officially recognized, and most people were too frightened to fill out the paperwork. How, I despaired, could I alone make management recognize the extent of the problem?

Meanwhile, I tried to hang onto the shredded fabric of my social life, although my body became harder to lug around. Friends sometimes dropped by on weekends when I had enough energy to visit. Although it aggravated my illness some, I occasionally went swimming at my neighborhood pool. Swimming improved a mild arthritis condition I'd had for a number of years, and it lifted my spirits. I would rise before the city had begun to shake off its sleep and shuffle over to the pool where I'd meet up with a company of 30-something-to-80-something-year-old women who also swam at 6:30 a.m. We had become friends over the years, perhaps because we were a small group foolish enough to be jumping into a pool together in the dark hours of the morning. We shared our thoughts and traded books, beginning the day with plenty of laughs.

Some people gave me advice when they heard about my health troubles, but no one offered encouragement. A stockbroker friend said he had hardly ever seen a large company face a problem head-on. He suggested it seems to be corporate nature to look the other way when a big problem comes along, hoping it will go away. He paused and sighed. "They'll probably try to make you the problem."

Another coworker told me he had suffered health problems from chemical fumes at a manufacturing plant and had seen the same dynamics before. "The companies don't want to give one inch," he explained, looking somber, "because they're afraid of what they might have to admit. Nothing's done to improve the situation because any action would acknowledge that there is a problem. They'll bring in experts to counter whatever the employees say. They'll get information about employees and use it against them. If any manager supports his staff, he'll get worn down by the battle." His flat voice expressed how hopelessly he viewed the situation. "I've never seen sick employees get anywhere – unless they have a union and a lot of money behind them."

"But the District will be different," I protested.

Trying to Tend a Garden

I savored those rare sunny days, the kind that sped by much too quickly, sandwiched as they were between pearly gray skies and bone-chilling dampness. Walking to the mailbox, I would feel the warm glow of sunlight across my face, making me want to dance. On this particular day, however, gray clouds moved slowly toward the sun. An ominous shade crept about the garden. I opened the mailbox to see a letter from the Washington State Department of Labor & Industries lying on top of the stack of envelopes like the first rumble of ominous thunder. Oh, no, I thought. My high spirits sank again, tied to this anchor. Mail from Labor & Industries always filled me with a cloying dread. Slowly I opened the envelope as if taking my time would help steel me for whatever lay inside. But I read the paper over and over, and it still didn't make much sense.

The Washington State Department of Labor & Industries (L&I) oversaw workers' compensation insurance for the state. This was the department to which I had sent my injury report more than a month ago. Here was Labor & Industries' response. They had accepted my injury claim. However, beneath that sentence, the word *protested* made me uneasy. I slammed the paper down to the ground and anger seeped through me. Minutes later, my calm restored, I called Lynn Eckholm, Workers' Compensation manager at the District, for help in translating the letter.

"Oh," she said, "L&I accepted your claim, making you eligible for partial reimbursement for workdays lost because of your injury. But the District then protested your claim, as the state gives them the right to do. They question whether your condition is really caused by the new building."

Until L&I could evaluate the situation, my claim would be held in limbo. By law, all employers had to carry workers' compensation insurance, which reimbursed employees injured on the job, regardless of who was at fault. L&I collected the insurance payments from employers and processed workers' compensation claims. Alternately, businesses could choose to manage their own workers' compensation insurance programs, with L&I acting as an overseer. The District had chosen the latter arrangement.

I replied to Lynn in disbelief that my problems clearly began with the building. The word "protested" continued to echo through my mind like a throbbing headache. A warm flush spread across my cheeks. Hadn't I been staggering around like Typhoid Mary ever since that first fateful day in the new building?

"It's common – we often protest injury claims," Lynn said, all cool and professional, like some news reporter announcing the day's stock report.

I felt stunned and angry and wondered whether the District's protest was more about keeping insurance costs low than about finding out the truth of my injury in an objective, open-minded way. I may as well have been standing in front of my burned-down house while an insurance agent justified denying paying me benefits. But hadn't my premium been paid year after year for situations like this?

It turned out that fewer than a dozen states recognized multiple chemical sensitivity as a legitimate claim for workers' compensation. Washington State was not one of them. The handful of workers with MCS who had won compensation for their injuries had done so because they'd developed a secondary, officially recognized illness such as asthma.

My only hope lay in L&I siding with me. How much clearer could my proof get? I had no history of a chemical-related illness. For eight years, I had worked at the District without complaining of building-related health problems while amassing more unused sick leave than almost anyone in the department. And my health problems began the very first day in the new building.

The letter reminded me that some District managers had asked me whether my health troubles weren't caused by my arthritis. But I had never had the symptoms before, I would tell them. Still, they had trouble believing a building could trigger so many problems. It was as if they thought having mild arthritis inoculated me from acquiring a new illness. That line of reasoning was something like deducing that someone with heart disease couldn't get cancer. Besides, I explained to them, many other sick staffers didn't have pre-existing health problems.

Meanwhile, word got out that Joan and I had filed injury claims. Some employees began dropping by Joan's office or calling me, mostly to complain about their own health troubles. One man said he felt as if he had a permanent case of the flu ever since we'd moved. Another told about how many staff members in his department were feeling sick, but how his boss had said he didn't want anyone making an issue of the illnesses. Joan and I began to feel like broken records as we told each person: The only way to get a response to your complaints is to file a claim. But few did.

Finally the air quality tests of the District building, which I had read about in the newspapers, were completed. The District-hired experts had made a small effort to measure some chemical fumes around Joan's and my offices but the tests didn't yield useful information. The available testing methods weren't sophisticated or refined enough to detect low-level contaminants. Besides, the scientific community lacked a good understanding of what amounts of chemicals could cause such health troubles or if breathing in a combination of them was more toxic than inhaling each chemical was on its own. Emily Conway from the Facilities Department called Joan and me to invite us to a meeting where the results of the testing would be presented. Other staff members concerned about air quality would also be invited. Since I obviously couldn't attend the meeting, because it was held in the new building, I asked Joan to take notes for me. Joan called me afterward with the report from the front lines.

"I'm so angry," she said. "Just before the meeting, I walked around the department, asking if anyone else was planning to go. No one had even heard about it. So immediately, four people decided to go."

"Maybe Emily told staff in other departments about the meeting," I said. "She said she was going to. Or maybe we've got more bureaucratic shenanigans on our hands?"

"Evidently Emily did not inform other departments either," Joan said. "Later on, when other staff heard about the meeting, they were furious they hadn't been told about it. When I walked into the auditorium, I was surprised to find only a few people – all of them managers. Everyone sat in chairs forming a circle: Todd Naiman, the consultant who did the testing; two managers from the Personnel Department; and Emily Conway from Facilities. That was it. So the five of us joined the circle. Todd started by saying his testing hadn't found anything specifically wrong with the building. He admitted that not much is known about what level of chemical fumes provokes illness. Then, you're going to love this part, he said the kind of health symptoms we've had can be psychological."

I groaned. "Didn't anyone pin him down and ask for specific proof?"

"Someone asked if something couldn't be done about her scratchy throats, headaches and ringing ears. Another wanted to know why the building smelled so much, and why the air was so heavy and stagnant. Then Emily explained that Facilities had considered baking out the building before staff moved in."

"What's baking out?" I wondered.

"It's a process used to speed up the release of chemicals from building materials and furnishings. They turn the heat way up, then vent the air outside. The problem, according to Emily, is that some people told them a bake-out can do more harm than good. Apparently it can release chemicals that might not otherwise outgas."

"But here's the best part, Anne." Joan paused, obviously deeply affected by what she was about to say. "Todd said the standard rule of thumb used in industry is that if no more than 20 percent of staff are getting sick from the workplace, you don't have a problem. The five of us just sat there, stunned."

The District lost no time in sending out a press release that declared its building problem-free. The absence of evidence was interpreted as proof enough that the building couldn't be causing health problems after all. From then on, whenever staff members complained of sickness, the managerial mantra became: "*We don't have a problem if no more than 20 percent of employees are sick.*" The irony was that, if we had taken a poll of staff, I suspected we probably had at least that many ill, based on the affected staff Joan and I knew of, and the fact that we didn't know everyone in the building.

The following day, I called Todd Naiman to discuss the testing further. "The air in my office feels stagnant," I said. "Do you think this might be part of the problem?"

"Stagnant is a relative term," he said. "Each person has a different perception of what stuffy is. There is no way to research it."

"Since our building is on the site of an old fish-processing company," I said, "could contaminants from their operations have leaked into the concrete foundation? Then the fumes might become problematic when you put a tightly sealed building over it."

"It's possible," he said. Then silence.

I persisted. "Someone from our Maintenance Department called to tell me that during the years the fish-processing plant sat vacant, hundreds of seagulls made it their home. Whenever Maintenance staff would clean up the concrete foundation, some would feel ill while they were there." I fidgeted with the telephone cord, sensing that the District-hired consultant might not be open to this idea. "Apparently some of the Maintenance staff say that they can still smell bird droppings in the new building. Do you think this might be one of the problems?"

"It's hard to say."

I may as well have been talking to a brick wall. My back stiffened, as if to gird myself to press on into this dense concrete jungle. I felt charged up by the challenge and yet utterly weary in one and the same moment.

"One of my healthcare providers gave me a medical study conducted by doctors at the Walter Reed Army Medical Center. It found that the allergen in pet birds and their droppings can cause health problems for their owners long after the birds are removed from their homes, even after extensive cleanup of the environment. They hypothesize that bird antigen may persist for long periods of time the way cat antigen does."

"Hmmmm," was the consultant's response. He wasn't going to research that idea either. I continued down my list of questions. Each concern was dismissed or ignored, but in an avalanche of good manners.

Afterward, I recounted the story to two people who had been members of indoor air quality committees at other organizations. They knew the District-hired consultant and they'd had similar experiences with him.

"I was really offended by Todd Naiman's presentation to my indoor air quality committee," one woman said. "Basically, his emphasis was on managing employees' outrage rather than on improving air quality." She pursed her lips in frustration. "He suggested that if you could pacify people by providing them with information, and by letting them feel a part of the process, you could control their anger."

I sat thinking of the double bind Todd must have been in. If he pursued air quality concerns too aggressively, companies might not hire him again or recommend him to others.

Later on, I would read of a paper presented at a healthy buildings conference where air quality experts suggested a plan for investigating sick buildings. At a minimum, they advised, in the first phase a questionnaire should be sent to employees, both those who were affected and those who were not. The ventilation system should be thoroughly evaluated, including measuring air flow, temperature, relative humidity, and carbon dioxide levels. The maintenance plan for the ventilation system should be reviewed. And the investigators should walk through the entire building to look for problems such as water-soaked building materials or misuse of janitorial cleaning fluids. In the second phase, airborne organic chemicals and microbials should be sampled if they are suspected of contributing to the complaints. At this point the District had resisted surveying employees, as I had suggested, and had not taken a thorough look at its ventilation system.

It was my turn to go to an occupational medicine specialist. I had located a doctor with a good reputation for his experience with chemical-related illnesses, and the District had agreed to pay the bill. The visit was technically called an independent medical exam by the workers' compensation system.

There I sat in the pale green waiting room, wondering if I would get more answers than Joan had. On my lap lay a stack of forms I'd been asked to fill out. *What are your symptoms? When did they start? Draw a diagram of your office environment, indicating where you sit.* On my drawing, I had added asterisks to show where other affected colleagues in my department sat.

"Anne Lipscomb?" Dr. William Lonsdorf said, extending his hand. He was tall with blond hair and wire-rimmed eyeglasses, and had the physique of someone who had played football in high school but whose contours had been softened by middle age. While Dr. Lonsdorf examined me, I gave him a pocket history of my problems. He listened carefully, his eyes poised on me like bright headlights while he pushed my limbs this way and that.

"You've just described problems common to people who work in tight buildings," he said. "The trouble is, very few unusual findings show up on blood work or in air quality testing so there's no point in ordering any tests. We don't know much about why this happens. Your symptoms don't resemble traditional allergies." He paused in thought. "I tend to favor the theory that it has a psychogenic origin – meaning you might have symptoms from airborne irritants in the beginning, but then you become psychologically conditioned to respond to odors. It's a difficult problem to research, though, because employers don't like having their workers studied for medical problems."

The physical exam was completed with no unusual findings. I sat down opposite the doctor. He scribbled notes in my chart as we talked, occasionally glancing at me through his glasses. "Some people report that their symptoms spread," Dr. Lonsdorf said, "and become triggered outside the building – as you are experiencing. This is typically called multiple chemical sensitivity, or environmental illness, although it is not a well-established diagnosis. For some reason it appears to affect women more than men."

What a relief, I thought. This is someone who knows something about my health problems. I slid to the edge of my chair, hopeful that he would have a remedy to prescribe.

Dr. Lonsdorf's voice grew intense as if he were lecturing a class. "But don't allow this to control your life." His blue eyes pierced through me. "There are people out there who get extreme and move to special communities for people with MCS. Don't let yourself get isolated like that."

He did offer some positive suggestions. Employees in sick buildings almost always got better when the ventilation was improved. Holding up my diagram of the Communications Department, I pointed out the cluster of cubicles where people were getting sick. He told me that the more people sitting in a space, the better the ventilation has to be because you have more people using the air.

"Might this explain why I can breathe more easily when I enter my director's office?"

The doctor nodded. Managers' offices – typically larger spaces with only one person in them – often have better-quality air. Dr. Lonsdorf offered to send his industrial hygienist to look at my workspace. Perhaps he would have some useful ideas. But weeks later, after walking through the building, the hygienist failed to find anything unusual.

The District then sent me to a second occupational medicine specialist for an independent medical exam. The physician came to a similar conclusion, that I had multiple chemical sensitivity, or MCS, and suggested a ventilation expert look at my office. He smoked like a chimney, the doctor laughed, but he was very knowledgeable about indoor air quality. This particular ventilation expert kept trying to retire, but his expertise remained too much in demand.

❧

Trying to keep my life from becoming engulfed by the new illness was growing more difficult. Whenever I wasn't working, I was usually lying down like a ship aimlessly drifting out to sea. What little energy I could muster had to be reserved for my job. Being housebound had come to seem like solitary confinement in prison. Before MCS, I often had longed for more solitude. Now, being forced into it, the experience seemed more hardship than pleasure. When Ted walked through the door in the late afternoon, I would greet him like a rambunctious puppy that had been cooped up in the house all day. Why in the past was it so difficult, I wondered, to find the right balance between time alone and time with others?

I began to talk on the telephone more often at night to assuage my loneliness. My friend Molly Geller grasped the effect the illness had on me. She responded creatively by calling me often at night and reading me bedtime stories. Hearing "Hi, it's Molly" on the telephone cheered me up immediately, like a warm security blanket pulled about my shoulders. "Are you ready for another story?" I could hear the rustling of turning pages.

"There's one in here about a man who placed a personal ad in the newspaper looking for a girl he had loved at summer camp 40 years before. Want to hear that one?" When Molly finished reading, we learned how he had indeed found her, and we marveled at some of life's coincidences. How nice to end the day on a note of wonder.

Heading to bed now had gotten complicated. I had become so sensitive to indoor pollutants that the bedroom window had to be partially open at night to prevent my feeling sicker. It could take 20 minutes to warm up after getting into bed. The room was that cold. "Anne, are you sure you need to have the window open?" Ted would ask, shivering and frustrated. "I can't sit and read in bed anymore." We had another bedroom next-door but I couldn't sleep there because the chemicals in its new mattress made me ill. At moments like these, we both felt trapped in this web-like illness. On the coldest nights, Ted would trudge off to the other room.

Ted and I decided to celebrate my birthday quietly that year, given all that we had going on. The night was so blustering that tree branches scraped against the window as we ate dinner and rain cascaded down the panes like a lush waterfall. When would spring arrive, I wondered, when would the flowers burst forth with the promise of new beginnings? I marveled at the food Ted had cooked, at the aroma of sizzling steak, at the crunchy roasted potatoes that yielded to creaminess with each bite. Mindful of wanting to keep the mood festive, I made an effort not to discuss my tedious health troubles even though they were often on my mind these days.

Ted handed me a large, cream-colored envelope. Inside, the inscription read, "This card entitles the bearer to six moves in the garden."

I loved it. What an inspired idea! I leaned over to kiss Ted, giggling with delight. When it came to my cherished garden, I forever wanted to move plants around. To me, the garden was like a palette and I was the artist-gardener. I would want to move this plant over there, to achieve a more dynamic color combination, or to bring that one over here, because it had grown too tall in its spot. The task of executing the moves often fell to Ted. Thus, his ingenious birthday gift for my roving garden: six moves, no questions asked.

∽

When the day came for ventilation expert John Webster to look at our communications offices, Joan once again took careful notes for me since I couldn't be there. The only other people at the meeting were a District lawyer, a Personnel Department manager, someone from the Facilities Department, and air quality expert Todd Naiman. Joan explained how our symptoms had come on suddenly, how the air in our new offices felt heavy and stagnant. Right away John held his hand up to the ceiling vent over my desk.

"There is hardly any air coming out," he said. "The air meant for Anne's office is going into the hallway instead." Air quality expert Todd Naiman said, well you learn something new every day. John had Joan hold her hand up to the various vents. She could hardly feel any air coming out of the vents in both of our offices, but in the hallway a forceful stream of air flowed out.

"And you need to get those damn grates off the vents," the ventilation expert said. "They're also reducing air flow and they're only used for decoration." John pointed out that sharp curves in our air ducts were cutting off air supply. They were probably designed that way, he surmised, to save money on materials. Had he been consulted when the building was designed, he would have suggested linear vents, the kind that directors had in their offices, for the entire staff. Still, John shrugged, Joan's and my type of illness was often psychosomatic.

Replacing the sharply curved air ducts would be expensive. Instead, John suggested that moveable slats be placed over the vents. That way we could at least direct the reduced air toward our desks.

Joan and I felt elated. Somebody had finally found a fixable problem; and the District had agreed to install the moveable slats. We had a good laugh at how air expert Todd Naiman hadn't thought of holding up his hand to the vents when I complained of stagnant air. The experts were beginning to remind me of a Laurel and Hardy comedy routine. Sometimes the specialists had trouble thinking in simple ways. We wondered what else they might be missing.

We had still more concerns. That John hadn't checked the building's entire ventilation system troubled us, especially because the building hardly had any walls. Sharply curved air ducts probably existed throughout the building where we knew others were feeling ill. We were disappointed by his solution to address the symptoms of the problem rather than tackling it at the root, by replacing the problematic air duct. And John's allusions to our illness often being psychosomatic dismayed us, especially when he had no proof.

The cadre of medical and air quality experts had all mentioned their psychosomatic theories – as if Joan and I, longtime employees with low absentee rates – had suddenly developed psychological problems that just happened to coincide with that first day in the new building. We were starting to feel that common sense wasn't always so common among the experts. The experts, who prided themselves on accuracy and objectivity, required hard, scientific evidence to say there was a problem, but they were surprisingly careless when implying that our health symptoms were psychological. One thing was for certain: When faced with a problem they couldn't fully explain, the specialists were masters at deflecting attention away from the limits of their knowledge onto the unfortunate sufferers with their psychosomatic theories.

Nevertheless, Joan and I took what help we could get. The moveable slats would be in by the time I resumed working in the office. Then, I silently pleaded, please let this be the cure. May I wake up from this surreal nightmare that has become my life to find it a distant memory. Visions of stormy pewter skies filled my head and then dissipated into shimmering rainbows. Desperately I clung to my hope. But the dream was not to be, at least for a long time.

❦

Back home, I finalized plans for expanding the garden. At first, Ted had been reluctant, knowing my creative penchant for getting carried away. He would have to do the physical part of the work, after all. But, I had explained, the garden had become so much more important to me now that I was housebound. The sight of shrubs and colorful flowers changing form inspired me with a range of feelings like a well-loved poem. When a plant came into bloom, I felt like an old friend had come to visit and I rejoiced in its tiny miracle.

Ted eventually warmed up to the idea, even embraced it. For now, I happily pored over garden books and catalogs, looking forward to the possibilities of future growth, and a future flowering.

Gifts from the Seas

Every once in a while, I still had the energy for socializing. One day my friend Melanie Gruber and I strolled along Lake Washington, her dog Buster trotting ahead of us, tugging at his leash. Because I had been so confined for such long hours, my senses needed some kind of renewal. Once I became open to the world outside again, I noticed I became aware so much more of the richness that surrounded me. Seeing things anew from within the perspective of illness, and then with the hope of recovery somewhere on the horizon, you think differently about the simple produce of daily life, the pace of time, and even the rhythms of the natural world.

Walking about with Melanie on this particular day, I could hear the pulse of the lake water lapping in a soothing tempo. A powdery light settled over the blue silhouette of mountains on the far side of the lake, and the clouds hung so low that they seemed to brush the worry from my shoulders. A curling mist rising from the water looked as if it belonged on the English moors. My frazzled thoughts were lulled into a deep peace by the sound of the water massaging the ragged shore. This was the kind of place, the sort of experience of the senses, that could console you and even change you if you took the time to pay attention.

Melanie, a small woman with clean-cut features, loved being in nature. We talked about how, with the advent of children, her much-loved outdoor pursuits had taken a back seat. Several men kicked a soccer ball under the nearby canopy of an oak tree as we passed by. Motorboats skimming the lake hummed in the distance. I laughed and told Melanie about my new office and my new-found illness. A startled look flashed across Melanie's face. "Boy, that's too frightening even to think about." Melanie then unleashed her dog and threw a stick into the water. Buster tore off in hot pursuit, as if he'd never seen a stick before. We watched as he paddled back toward us, stick clenched in his teeth, looking thoroughly proud and delighted. The repetition of our casting off and his retrieving back brought me a strange sense of comfort.

Afterward, as we climbed into Melanie's station wagon, she said, "I think I know someone who has had an illness like yours. He found help through Ayurveda medicine. Let me know if you ever want to talk to him." I thanked her and appreciated that she had left her offer open-ended. Someday I might take her up on it. Just then life felt too overwhelming. But the day proved a welcome return to normal social life and seemed to promise future returns.

∽

It felt good to be back. Colleagues decorated my office, a "Welcome Back!" sign adorned my wall, and chocolate bars and candies lay nestled in a purple basket on my desk. All day a steady stream of people stopped by to see me, even to hug me, and to express relief that I looked so well. The three months of working at home were finally over and my symptoms were 90 percent gone. Most significantly, the moveable slats had been installed and Joan was feeling better. At last the problem seemed behind me. More than five months had passed since we'd moved to the new building. I wore my hope and positive thinking to the office like a suit of armor so it might protect me from any more harm. My doctor had sent the District a letter suggesting I start with one hour a day in the building, increasing gradually as my health permitted. They had agreed to the plan.

A new communications director, my fifth boss in eight years, introduced herself and shook my hand. Nancy Murdoch had joined the District only weeks ago. Her job would not be easy. In an age where the media tended toward adversarial investigative reporting, where increasingly sophisticated community groups fought to make the District more accountable to the public, and where the agency had to

54

operate like a business in a highly competitive industry, Nancy was going to find herself hard pressed to satisfy everyone. Most people lasted only a few years in the position.

Despite all the seeming improvements, with each day back in the building, my symptoms worsened. They didn't just reappear; they grew more severe, and additional problems cropped up. I despaired, feeling as if I couldn't take the situation getting any worse. Now – in addition to the nausea, dizziness, and headaches – my hands and feet stung as if they were pricked by a thousand needles. I began to get insomnia; at night I would lie awake, wired, as if I had drunk 16 cups of coffee, my body buzzing like a hot electric cable. Persistent sore throats began to plague me. I struggled to breathe, feeling like an elephant sat on my chest, and wondered if I might be developing asthma. Nevertheless, I pressed on, disciplining myself to disregard the cacophony banging against my quivering body and increasing my time to three hours a day in the building. All the while I hoped that somehow my body would adjust.

I searched for solutions desperately. Nancy agreed to my proposal of sitting in a vacant office at the other end of the building. Some roving employees had reported feeling better in that area than they had in our department. One day she and I sat talking on the balcony overlooking Elliott Bay. I suggested ways I could get work done from home since I still worked part of the day there. I emphasized that I wanted the arrangement to work for both of us. Please, I said, let me know if you think it doesn't work, and I can propose other ideas. Nancy sat staring at me, stony-faced, her body tensed, her jaw trembling slightly. Suddenly she burst out, "I need to know exactly what you're working on. I want a full account." In my mind, I cursed the bad luck at having a new director begin at a time like this. She wasn't likely to be as understanding as someone who knew me well and trusted my work ethic.

My colleagues accommodated me by holding weekly staff meetings outdoors on the balcony when weather permitted. I made sure to get plenty of rest when not working. Yet my condition steadily deteriorated as if I had plunged over a cliff. Making matters worse, the chemical illness now exacerbated my pre-existing arthritis so much that the long walk from the parking garage to the office brought on searing pain. My feet and knees felt swollen like sausages, and my spine burned like a high fever. My doctor arranged for me to be eligible for the District's handicapped parking spots located next to the building. But when I arrived at work, all designated parking places were already taken. I talked to the Facilities Department about my predicament. They, in turn, consulted with Harris Downing, the District lawyer about to be assigned my workers' compensation case. The District already met legal requirements for the number of disability parking spots, Harris said. They weren't required to do anything more.

The next morning, I drove to the parking area again. This time I was in luck. There was one spot still open. But before I could pull in, another car zipped past me and slid into the space in the nick of time. Lawyer Harris Downing emerged from the car, hopping along on crutches like an injured rabbit, due to a temporary injury. I sat dumbfounded, wondering how he could have given his strictly legal opinion about my parking dilemma when he knew firsthand what it was like to have to count on using one of the disabled parking spots. When I got to my office, weak and throbbing from the long walk, I bumped into Joan and told her of the morning's event. What do you think will be more effective, I joked to Joan: appeal to Harris' decency or get to work earlier so he can see what it's like to hop up and down the city streets to reach the office?

Joan smiled like a Cheshire cat. "I'd get here early if I were you." I threw my hands up in the air for dramatic effect.

❧

On the spur of the moment, Ted was invited to join his father on a trip to Paris to visit his sister and her family. At first he didn't think he should leave with all that was going on. But I insisted I could manage alone. I felt pleased to see him go off since we both loved traveling so much. He shouldn't pass up the opportunity. The day before Ted left, he asked again, "Are you sure you'll be all right?" his eyebrows arched, head tilted slightly to the side. A flurry of suitcase packing ensued. Passport checked, treats for our French nieces and nephew, telephone calls to reschedule dental appointments. Ted was off. The next day while reaching into my sock drawer, I pulled out a small package wrapped in silver paper. Inside lay the most recent compact disc of one of my favorite music groups. That same day a card arrived from Ted, mailed from Seattle before he left. Several days later I stumbled upon an envelope tucked into a cereal bowl: a gift certificate to a fabric store to feed my passion for sewing. It was gestures like this, I thought, that made all the difference.

But not everyone was so supportive. By now my friend Melanie had grown skeptical of my health problems. When she came over to borrow a book one day, as she was leaving she said, "The insomnia you're having – maybe it's because you're letting yourself get too upset about your health." She spoke deliberately but sweetly, as if to soften the effect of her words, running her hand through her thick hair. "The effect of stress doesn't get taken into consideration enough."

"Of course stress can keep you from sleeping," I replied, dismayed. "But so can chemical exposure. I see the connection regularly because when I go to a place like the hardware store or spend time in a hot tub, I barely sleep all night." Melanie's chin tightened, her eyes glazed over while she looked past me, as if rehearsing what to say next. "It would help to get your mind off of yourself. Have you thought of taking up some hobbies? Maybe you'd like to go on a hike with me and some friends sometime. It might do you some good."

She turned abruptly and walked out the door. I stood there taken aback, feeling like a native in some foreign land who had just been visited by a missionary – not the genuinely loving, compassionate kind, but the arrogant, self-righteous type. Without understanding my own country, culture, and circumstances, she had presumed to know what was best for me. From that point on, whenever Melanie proposed get-togethers or outings, her invitations gave the impression that I was being targeted as a social service improvement project rather than chosen for my company.

⁓

At the District, other employees quietly despaired as they nursed along their own health problems. The Facilities Department gave David Hall, the manager in the Marketing Department who had been experiencing shortness of breath, an air purifier for his office, but it had not helped.

Then the District sent David to Dr. Lonsdorf, the same occupational medicine specialist I had seen. David reported that Dr. Lonsdorf mentioned he had seen other staff from the District and eventually told him the new building might have caused his health symptoms. He chose his words very carefully, though, and was very guarded about giving an opinion. Dr. Lonsdorf didn't suggest any course of action or that David get out of the building.

Helen Smith, in the Equal Opportunity Department, found her health worsening enough that she filed an injury report. Because of the bad headaches she had been having, her doctor took a small piece of an artery out of her head because he thought an artery was closing down. Once a headache was so bad – she thought her head might explode – that she went to a hospital emergency room. There they ordered a CAT scan, neurological tests, everything, but they did not know what was going on. Apparently her sediment rate was five or six times higher than it should be but she did not have an infection.

Later on, she started noticing blood in her urine. She got asthma for the first time in her life and her body was aching all over. The strangest things have been happening, Helen said. Her nose was getting sensitive to smells. She had a couch for years and never had a problem with it, but now whenever her body touched it, she would get a rash. She said she tried to suggest to the doctor that her new office might have something to do with this cluster of symptoms, but his attitude was, no, medicine doesn't recognize such an illness. He said he would have to look for something in the book. So he just kept testing and testing with no result.

A slew of other complaints continued from a number of employees and visitors: headaches, nausea, vomiting, frequent colds, bronchitis. There were other disturbing problems. The person responsible for watering the plants in our building told my colleague that, for some strange reason, she was having trouble keeping plants alive in our Communications Department.

Why wouldn't people come forward and speak up, I wondered? Many admitted health concerns to their closest friends or to Joan and me, then denied them to others. Why would a person gamble on something as important as health? No doubt fears of retaliation, or of coming forward without a doctor's support, played a role. But this didn't seem to be the whole reason. Whatever the explanation, Joan and I suspected that even if the District sent out a questionnaire to employees, many wouldn't respond truthfully.

I had learned that people don't always speak up even when there is an obvious chemical exposure after I read about a chemical factory that accidentally exploded in Italy in *The Pendulum and the Toxic Cloud*. When the plant exploded, a white plume shaped like an inverted cone rose into the sky, turned into a cloud, and settled over part of the town. Birds that had been flying through the cloud died immediately and dropped to the ground. Within two days, small animals were dying. Townspeople who had been outside at the time quickly developed obvious symptoms like sores on their faces, arms and legs. The amount of chemicals that had been released was significant enough that part of the community was evacuated to another town, where temporary housing was set up. Eventually many townspeople developed illnesses known to be linked to dioxin. Despite this knowledge, and the fact that residents saw the explosion and watched animals dying, some still refused to believe the situation was serious. A few even broke through fences that had been erected around their homes, to sneak back and get their personal belongings, leaving a trail of dioxin in the process. Apparently they believed the government had overestimated dioxin's hazards, or that health problems wouldn't happen to them.

After seven months in the new building, and despite mounting health problems, the District continued with a "let's not panic the employees" approach. A few managers quietly acknowledged that the District had air quality troubles, but their conclusion was, "We just don't know what else to do about it." I found it curious that an organization as sophisticated as the District couldn't figure out what to do. Savvy business people could be quite naive when there was a problem they didn't want to face, or when it wasn't a priority.

Joan called someone at a local agency responsible for the Washington Industrial Safety and Health Act. She asked if the inspection staff would do a thorough test of our building, not the limited spot-checking that had been performed to date. But they told her that because of a recent reorganization, inspections had been transferred to L&I – the department that would pay out compensation claims if they discovered a problem. Stunned by this apparent conflict of interest, Joan called L&I anyway. A bureaucrat there told her that an inspection would have to be requested by someone at the District who had authority to take action; but in any case, he said, they probably wouldn't find anything specifically wrong, and L&I's testing was running three months behind schedule. Joan still thought it worth a try. Because our Communications Department director Nancy sat on the Building Committee, and since we wanted to work within the system if possible, Joan asked Nancy to have the Building Committee request L&I do an inspection. I'll bring it up with them, Nancy replied. But she never did.

Meanwhile, District-wide, staff members were being asked to work more productively. Managers enthusiastically talked about improving the quality of work by empowering their employees; staff should be respected and their ideas listened to, they exclaimed, to help foster a sense of ownership in the organization and enhance their work.

Nancy and I were meeting weekly in addition to our staff meetings. One day Nancy sat in my office in her stylish black skirt and white knit blouse, a silver lace pin on her collar. I told her about my projects. "Uh-huh," she said, her eyes flitting about. A pause. She had a way of acknowledging what people were saying without conveying what she thought or felt. "Could you attend a meeting on Monday and help me with an upcoming Pacific Rim conference?" Nancy asked, staring at me. Yes, I said, I would budget that meeting into my three hours a day in the building. District staff were asking for a reference booklet on international trade facts and figures, Nancy continued. Could I put something together? Of course, that is a project I could easily do from home.

Despite my resolve, my symptoms continued their downward spiral, sucking me uncontrollably into quicksand. Whether or not there were further air quality investigations would not matter because they would be too late. I didn't need tests to tell me that my workplace attacked me like a powerful toxin and that it stubbornly hammered away at me, one blow after another, even when I wasn't in the building. Two-and-a-half months after my third attempt to work in the building, and eight months into the new office, I was forced to take a medical leave. My symptoms had become so severe that I could barely function. In addition to my usual symptoms, my chest cavity burned like an out-of-control forest fire. Breathing, laughing, coughing and sneezing triggered sharp, stabbing sensations that made me wince. I felt weak all over. I was a flickering candle about to blow out. The fatigue was on a scale that I'd never known before. Just doing something as simple as keeping my foot pressed on the accelerator while driving took all of the effort that I could summon. The nights no longer provided a respite to recharge myself either, because I could only doze lightly. Dragging my leaden self from a rumpled bed each morning, I often couldn't imagine how I was going to make it through the day. I was crushed at the thought of taking a medical leave though fearful of my quick physical demise. I wondered how long it would take me to climb out of this abyss. A large chunk of my life, it seemed, had suddenly fallen into the sea. And having a condition that was so little understood was one of the loneliest feelings I have ever known.

At home, I felt like a refugee suddenly thrown into some foreign, barren land. My heart ached for my homeland, for the comfort of the known and the ordinary. That first week of medical leave, I answered a knock at my front door to find a deliveryman holding a cardboard box: a surprise package from some colleagues in the Communications Department. Inside a round box were several packets wrapped in gold tissue. There was Anne Morrow Lindbergh's *Gifts from the Sea*, colorful polished stones, dried strawberries, and a handmade card. Also several employees from various departments throughout the District had generously donated their sick leave to me, since I would no longer draw a salary once my own sick leave ran out. Tears burst at the corners of my eyes, especially since some of the donors didn't even know me. Despite my misery, I felt happy that my little world was populated with such generous and compassionate people.

Some Small Fireworks

Were you to have walked past our home, you might have wondered what in the world was going on. New clothes would be draped over the porch rail, flapping in the breeze, left outside until their chemical smells dissipated. Opened magazines littered the deck, airing out after their perfumed pages had been torn out. An ironing board might be protruding from an upstairs window while I pressed clothes, wearing a facemask. In the middle of winter you might have found our doors and windows wide open to let in fresh air. MCS had made us a bit stranger but also resourceful.

Fortunately, Ted and I could usually laugh about how odd life had become. The house was beginning to look like a flea market, Ted remarked. He would pick up a piece of clothing and ask me, "How much are you charging for this?" Or I would sometimes quip, "Ted, I'm thinking of changing my name to The Princess and the Pea. What do you think?" Being sensitive to so many chemicals meant that something was inevitably going to set me off. I felt as if I were clinging to slippery rocks, hanging above a turbulent sea while trying to climb to safety; just when I gained a firmer foothold, another wave came crashing in, making things so much more slippery.

I would set up the Christmas tree – an artificial one that had been airing out for a year because I now reacted to evergreen trees – and I'd sit down to admire the sight. Soon a sickening smell would hang in the air and I'd realize the tree lights were heating up the plastic needles. All right, I'd say to myself, disappointed, no lights this year. I'd try to let the frustration roll off my shoulders while bringing a portable air filter into the room. Then I'd sit down, prop my feet up on the coffee table, and compliment myself on another problem resolved with minimal drama. These were the rhythms of living with MCS. And these were the daily chores.

Occasionally, there was a knock at the door. Our boarder, living in the basement bedroom, would want to know if she could use our telephone to call her boss since hers wasn't working. But our cordless telephone still reeked of her fragranced shampoo from the last time she borrowed it. Washing the telephone hadn't worked, nor had letting it air out. So all week I'd been making a mad dash upstairs to answer the telephone because that one didn't smell. I would ask the boarder if I could make the call for her and when I did, her boss would get testy and demand to know why our boarder wasn't making the call herself.

Just as I would sit down to recuperate from this latest challenge to my body's equilibrium, a curl of smoke would drift past my nose. The toaster oven was on fire. My days sometimes took the theme of a television sitcom. If I had to watch it on a screen, I'd think the show was stupid and farfetched. Real life, I'd say to myself, wasn't like this. And it certainly wasn't comedy to me.

Somehow, through all the daily challenges, I learned to cultivate a life which minimized the factors that triggered my symptoms. My first priority was to reduce indoor pollution. The first year, I used a guidebook for low-toxic living, slowly working my way through the suggestions until I was able to tolerate being inside. The book was Debra Lynn Dadd's *Nontoxic, Natural, & Earthwise*. It became a kind of daily bread, a sort of bible for me. I started with the bedroom, where we spent about one-third of our day. At first the task seemed daunting: Mattresses were laced with pesticides and flame inhibitors, bed sheets contained dyes and other chemicals, closet shelves and furniture made with plywood or particle board were held together with glues, and clothes had chemicals in them. Quick solutions often eluded me. For instance, I couldn't relax just because we slept on natural fiber sheets; 25 percent of all insecticides are used on cotton production alone, so even cotton sheets contain pesticide residues. Out went the linens, and in came organic sheets; out went polyester-filled pillows and in came down-filled ones. This was only the beginning.

Ted brushed a vapor sealant onto particleboard and plywood to seal in their gases. We discovered particleboard everywhere – in the interior of wood kitchen cabinets, closet shelves, desks, furniture. "I just wish," Ted lamented, paintbrush poised in his hand, "that I had something to show for all of this work. The place doesn't look any different!" We stood outside on the deck. Shelves lay scattered about, as if a tornado had blown through, the contents of kitchen drawers spilled over in the corner. I felt guilty that I couldn't help. Even though the sealant was low-toxic, its smell sickened me until it dried.

I was dismayed to learn that in the shower most of us wash and lather ourselves with an array of chemicals, present in soap, shampoo, and tap water, easily absorbed because our skin pores are open. Whenever I stumbled onto new information like this, it made me want to lie down and take a nap. Nevertheless, I would press on. In went a screw-on shower filter, after which the water lost its swimming-pool odor. Out went soaps and lotions with chemicals and fragrances; in came natural, unscented toiletries. And in the bathroom, as in the rest of the house, we changed to natural cleaning products like vinegar and baking soda, after I discovered that many cleaning products are registered with the EPA as pesticides.

But we couldn't stop there: We had to make changes in the garden, too. When pesticides are sprayed outdoors, they travel indoors by way of shoes and pets. And that was unacceptable if you consider that the most common pesticides for gardens contain some of the same agents used in chemical warfare. Pesticides can cause problems like peripheral nerve or brain damage. Besides, using them is like wielding a sledgehammer when a screwdriver might do. After switching to natural products, I was delighted to discover that our garden grew just as well as before.

Despite all the changes, our house had to be aired out weekly to keep the indoor pollution level down. In the winter, if Ted wasn't at work, he would hole up in his study, windows closed, snuggled in a down parka, while I turned off the furnace and threw open the doors and windows in the rest of the house. He tried to make the best of the situation, but it was like camping out in winter. Sometimes our breath hung heavy in the air, the house was that cold. The airing would last for a half-hour, but it could take hours for the house to return to a comfortable temperature.

Changing our diet required more effort. The task was more complex than simply buying organic food, because organic items weren't always available. David Steinman's *Diet for a Poisonous Planet* was helpful. It lists the average amounts of pesticides in food, which taught me how to make healthier food choices. Chemical levels in food vary widely, depending on how much a particular crop needs to be sprayed and how easily it absorbs pesticides. Most conventionally grown bananas, for instance, do not contain pesticide residues once they are peeled, while peanut butter has an average of 183 residues; animal foods with higher fat contents, such as butter, ice cream, and meat, each typically carry over 100 different pesticide residues, more than in most fruits and vegetables. I struck a compromise. Organic food or food that was low in pesticides comprised the mainstay of my diet. The rest I ate very occasionally, though savoring each bite.

When I adopted an organic diet, Ted would buy organic food for me but not himself. He wasn't ready to change, he told me. When I drank a glass of organic milk, he would ask how it tasted, a hint of suspicion in his voice. Years before, I'd had a similar bias about organic products. It's twisted logic, I now realized, to think milk doesn't taste as good because it doesn't have chemicals or antibiotics in it. Then Ted read a book about an entire farming family that became chemically ill from pesticides routinely sprayed on food crops. The next time I helped him unpack the groceries, everything I pulled out of the bag was organic. I smiled and held my tongue.

Ted and I even changed the way we stored food: Out went plastic containers leaching chemicals, and in went cellophane bags and glass jars. Interestingly, after we made the changes, Ted noticed he got colds and the flu less often.

❧

With all of our new purchases, our living expenses were mounting. In addition to filing a claim with the workers' compensation program, I had also applied for disability benefits through Morgan Thomas, the District's private insurance company. It was separate from the workers' compensation program. Morgan Thomas paid claims for general medical disabilities. If L&I later found my illness to be work-related, Morgan Thomas would discontinue paying me benefits and would be reimbursed.

One afternoon a Mr. Frank Padden with Morgan Thomas telephoned to tell me he was managing my claim. Not long into the conversation, Mr. Padden said he didn't believe in sick-building syndrome unless there had been a specific incident, like a chemical spill.

"We've even had employees at Morgan Thomas complain of indoor air," Mr. Padden said. "But although tests showed that our ventilation system pulls in some bus exhaust from the street, our offices were found to be fine."

How were acceptable levels of chemicals determined? I asked. And was the combined effect of multiple chemicals mingling in the air taken into consideration? Mr. Padden dismissed my questions. "Everyone likes to have nice furniture and offices," he said. Nevertheless, after sending me for a medical evaluation, Morgan Thomas approved my claim. The payments did not reimburse me for my entire salary, but any bit helped.

Meanwhile, I continued marching on, making other changes to my life. Often I wore a cotton facemask fitted with a charcoal insert when going to places like the hardware store or to healthcare appointments. I loathed wearing a mask, but it was better than getting sicker. The mask made me quite the sight. One cashier once raised his arms when he saw me and joked, "I give up. Take the cash!" A child in a store tugged at his mother's sleeve one day, saying, "Mom, look, it's a doctor!" Wearing sunglasses with the mask really brought out its inherent charm. When my brother saw me like this, he hooted, as only a brother could get away with, "Anne, you look like a fruit fly!"

An air purifier in my car cut down on pollution. Since I didn't have air conditioning and the car windows had to be closed, in summer I would arrive places in a burning stupor, my clothes plastered to my back. This was the only time I appreciated that Seattle summers are so short. To work on the computer, I had to buy a glass and metal box to place over the machine, to exhaust its fumes; and I wrapped a new plastic computer keyboard shelf in cellophane because, even after it had aired out on the deck for months, the smell nauseated me.

Fragrances turned out to be a stubborn problem. In a few short generations, we've grown so accustomed to perfumes in everything that we don't even notice them. At first, my severe reaction to perfume puzzled me; it seemed like such a harmless substance, after all. But I learned that most fragrances are essentially solvents mixed with other chemical compounds, and many are made from the same ingredients found in pesticides, plastics, and paints. The perfume and fragrance industries are unregulated. The National Institute for Occupational Safety & Health had identified 884 toxic chemical substances used in the cosmetics and perfume industries. Many of these substances were capable of causing cancer, birth defects, central nervous system disorders, breathing and allergic reactions and multiple chemical sensitivities.

Perfume bothered me so much that, when getting together with friends, I asked them not to wear it. Someone wearing perfume reeked as if she had been sprayed by a skunk. Holding my nose couldn't stop the sickening aroma either. Fragrances emitted by the laundry soap in people's clothes bothered me, too; it smelled as bad as turpentine. Although people readily agreed not to wear fragrances, they didn't realize how many scents they were still trailing from shampoo, toiletries, and laundry soap. Even when washed in unscented detergent, clothes can retain fragrances the same way they can retain cigarette smoke. Clothes laundered with fabric softeners and dryer sheets were especially noxious. How I loathed asking friends to shed their fragrances. It made me feel self-conscious and embarrassed, but the alternative was worse.

❧

Summers grew more special because so many activities were held outside where I usually tolerated the air better. Ted and I entertained spontaneously on the deck and went to outdoor restaurants on little-trafficked streets. Nights and weekends were enlivened by dance performances, theater, and concerts in local parks. Life felt almost normal again, except activities I had once taken for granted now gave me far more pleasure, contrasted as they were with a life full of deprivation. Simple events that had once been fun now had become downright exhilarating.

One Fourth of July weekend, my friend Molly Geller suggested going to a small-town parade followed by a picnic and fireworks. Arriving an hour before the parade, we set up chairs on a curb on Main Street, where the sidewalks were already thick with people. A scent of sunscreen permeated the air. I reached into my bag for some buffered vitamin C powder, which dissolved in water and helped me deal with chemical reactions. All at once we heard the local high school band's rum-pa-pa notes in the distance. The parade had begun. Little girls in pink tutus twirled past us, followed by Cub Scout troops decked out in freshly pressed uniforms. When gleaming antique cars drove by, I raised my mask to my face at the odor of their exhaust. Molly leaned over to point out a pirate float.

Despite the momentary spells of nausea, I was spellbound. Compared with my barren, housebound life, the parade was a titillating explosion of colors, textures and sounds. I hadn't had so much stimulation in months and felt drunk with pleasure. The moment made me realize what a vacuum my life was increasingly becoming. Afterward, we ate our picnic in a park watching two fire departments battle each other with fire hoses. Both teams of firemen, swaddled in helmets and bulky orange suits, lifted fire hoses into the air. The goal was to use the force of water to push a ball suspended on a metal line to the opponent's side. Streams of water sprayed off the ball in every direction. Suddenly the firemen turned their hoses toward the crowd, their water arching over us. Children squealed in delight, running in circles and holding their arms out to catch the ocean spray. And there was more. The day ended on a dramatic note with a brilliant fireworks show. Neon streaks burst upon a silver sky that melted into pink just above the craggy Olympic Mountains. It was the best Fourth of July I could remember. I wanted to hold that moment in the palm of my hand, in my mind's eye, forever. Would the day, I wondered, have been quite so special in my former life? I don't think it would have.

Toward the end of the summer, dread would creep upon me. Dread for the fall, dread for the isolation it would bring. Activities would be curtailed. Sadly, fall had once been one of my favorite seasons. Fantasies of moving to a warmer climate where life could be lived outdoors most of the year soon followed this dread. But uprooting Ted's and my life, leaving our community and longtime friends, never seemed worth it.

Of all the symptoms MCS triggered, perhaps the most unsettling was cognitive impairment. I'd always had good verbal skills. Words came quickly and fell off my tongue. Now my mind felt like a gray-pasty mush. To articulate what I wanted to say, often I had to grope for the right words. Sometimes the words seemed to dribble out of me, as if searching for someone to string them together into an intelligible sentence. It felt as if my head was constantly swollen, pressure pushing out the sides and top – as if I had arthritis of the brain. Head massages brought relief, but they didn't clear my mind. Tests showed my verbal ability and short-term memory were low for someone of my academic background. If I was exposed to increased levels of chemicals or went for a brisk walk, my mind would feel like thick pea soup for the rest of the day. This change wasn't noticeable to others, although some friends told me I was talking more slowly. The brain problems left me especially vulnerable. If I was dizzy or nauseous, at least I could count on my brain to help me make good decisions, like about what doctor to consult. But if my mind wasn't all there – the prospect was daunting.

One time I started making dinner on the stovetop, forgetting that 15 minutes before I had put a casserole in the oven. Once, after cooking, I untied my apron but forgot to take it off. As I left the kitchen, the apron strings got twisted around my ankles and I stumbled. Another time I was talking to Ted and a neighbor, and complete gibberish came out of my mouth. But it was the day I forgot a heavy-duty pot on the stove when I realized what dire straits I was in. It melted down to a hunk of metal that clung to the burner before the thought of it swam up to my memory. I began to leave reminder notes everywhere. And I set timers. Sometimes I couldn't even remember why the buzzer had been set. The house sounded like a symphony of beeping when they were all going off at once.

✂

Making all these changes was tough on Ted. I could sympathize with him. The situation was exasperating to me, but at least the effort changed my life for the better. For Ted, the changes merely presented another burden without hope of improving his lot. But what he found hardest was not having a choice in most of the decisions.

The illness placed unprecedented pressure on our relationship. I had been sick for more than a year and there was no end in sight. There was so much I didn't understand then, that wouldn't come out until much later. When I asked Ted how he was feeling about the effects of my illness, he would admit to being frustrated about things like not having more choices with all of the changes in our lifestyle, but he would say that being with me was still worth living with my health troubles.

It would be years before I would realize that we did not do a good job of tending to both of our experiences, and how depressing the illness was for Ted as well as for me. Most couples facing a serious sickness do not do this well either, but they often get away with it because the illness resolves itself or improves significantly within a few years. At the time, I saw that Ted wasn't up to taking care of me, although he could certainly be tender and thoughtful in moments. I felt like we were each doing the best we could under terribly challenging circumstances. Occasionally I would think about the two of us consulting a therapist, but the cost was hard to justify with my mounting health bills.

So we struggled along and tried to get creative. I proposed more activities outdoors – picnics in the mountains, strolls along the lake, bird watching. We cultivated other interests like making and editing home movies. Since my ability to get out was limited, Ted sometimes went by himself to see films or have dinner with friends; occasionally he took vacations with his family. It was a relief; his life shouldn't be restricted. I volunteered to do things like make telephone calls or shop by mail. It was amazing how much could be done by telephone. One day I told Joan Bell how frustrating it was that our washing machine had broken and I wasn't well enough to go buy a new one. Why don't you just call Sears, she suggested, and order one over the telephone. What a great idea, I thought. After all, shopping for a washing machine wasn't like picking out a sofa – I didn't have to see the contraption in person. From then on, I became the queen of shopping by telephone.

Curiously, I noticed that going into stores less diminished my consumer cravings. My new life revealed to me how seductive exposure to material goods can be and how, sometimes, getting more just makes you want more. All too often, merely seeing things for sale made me want to own them. We are a nation of indefatigable shoppers. Americans spend about seven times more time shopping than Western Europeans. When I did venture out from my monastery life to a department store, all the while rushing to pick up what I needed before my symptoms flared up, all of a sudden I saw all kinds of goods I was sure I needed, things I hadn't needed a half-hour earlier. A new appliance for the kitchen. Or a blouse that looked so much nicer than the one in my closet. Thank goodness I had to make a quick exit. It was a blessing in disguise, considering my limited budget as an unemployed person.

Around Ted, my health updates were kept to a minimum. The subject could easily have engulfed us. Ted was struggling with issues different from mine, like feeling guilty about complaining about my illness. Also, my medical leave was costing us money. In addition to Ted's salary, we had my income from the District's private disability insurance and from taking a boarder into our basement bedroom. Still, the sum total was nowhere near what my salary and benefits had been when I was working. Just thinking about what MCS was doing to Ted's life put pressure on me, as did making an effort to be sociable around him on my sicker days. Sometimes I wondered if he wouldn't be better off without me, and I without him. Once we adjusted to the changes – as much as we could – life was fine, though not as lively. But we couldn't get completely around the fact that as my world grew smaller, so did Ted's.

There were times when I feared our marriage couldn't survive the problems MCS brought into our lives. Most of us who get married at a tender age don't give much thought to the in-sickness-or-in-health part of the marriage vows. Neither Ted nor I could have guessed something like MCS would crop up in our lives. How could Ted have known what it would be like to come home day after day to someone who could only say it had been a tough day on the couch?

I tell you, the thought that the two of us might not endure was awful. Sometimes I couldn't stop myself from wondering and worrying. Losing Ted would be traumatic. He had brought so much joy to my life. Additional worries cropped up, like if it happened, how could I support myself? Even if I could work, would there be periods when the MCS would flare up, incapacitating me? Where would I live? Paying the mortgage would be prohibitive, and if I found a housemate, what were the chances that a person would go along with all of the restrictions I had to endure? The thought of choosing a housemate with MCS – who, like me, was sick a lot and home all the time – was hardly appealing. One sick person in a household was enough. These thoughts would reel through my head on the darkest days.

☙

Years into the illness, when enough losses had piled up, seeking advice from a therapist seemed a worthwhile expense. I longed to find a way to thrive despite my illness, not just merely to survive. That's when a friend recommended Sally Newell, a psychological counselor experienced with chronic illness. I would come to appreciate her combination of keen intuition and rigorous thinking. From the first appointment in Sally's bright, airy office, I could see I should have gone to her – sometimes with Ted – as soon as I had gotten sick. Most people don't possess the repertoire of skills and insights needed for a condition like MCS. Coping with an ongoing illness, I learned, requires ongoing support. Best of all, Sally, a woman with short gray hair who laughed easily, had personal knowledge of sick-building syndrome. Her own office had once triggered health problems for her.

A partially opened, seven-foot-high window dominated Sally's high-ceilinged office. Oak bookcases and a desk lined one side of the room, framed by an arching rubber tree. I sat in a low-slung blue canvas chair next to the open window. Fortunately, with my mask on and outside air coming in, I could tolerate the space. Sally sat opposite me, dressed in a colorful printed blouse and skirt, listening to my story.

"That's funny," she said. "I've heard several other people mention that staff are having health problems in the District headquarters." A pause.

"The building I'm in," she explained, nursing a mug of tea in her lap, "used to be a school. I moved into this space while a developer was renovating the building into offices. For two years, I felt fine working here. Then they sealed the building." She pointed to the large opened window next to me. "It started to smell right away. I began feeling ill – respiratory problems, labored breathing, my eyes draining and weepy. Things got bad enough that I couldn't work in my office."

"Were other people in the building having problems?" I asked. I was inspired, talking to someone who had recovered from building-related illness. Outside the window, a drenching rain had started. People ran toward the building pulling raincoats over their heads, a couple huddled under the shadow of their umbrella. After a few minutes, the rain had glazed the pavement a deep, rich black. Then, just as abruptly, it stopped. It was a quintessential spring day.

"I interviewed people in nearby offices and was amazed at how many people were experiencing symptoms. Some had nausea and headaches. People were reluctant to say anything even though they were leasing their offices. So I met with the building manager. I told him I wasn't complaining but that I wanted a review of the situation." She shifted in her chair. "There is so much fear about lawsuits these days. The issue, I told him, was to see if we could identify the offending compound." Sally was silent a moment, as if trying to recall what happened. "In the end, management spent two months overhauling the duct system. Two to three weeks later, I felt totally better. I've been fine ever since."

She smiled, looking pensive. "When you have an ongoing illness, you have to work much harder at creating a good life. You almost have to make a superhuman effort. So much happens without effort when people are healthy. You're inhabiting a different world."

I was intrigued. No one had spelled this out so clearly to me before. But it made sense. "How do you go about doing that?"

"With lingering illness, you have to be a better person – more conscious, working through your issues more. You have to be better rather than superior." Sally looked at me and thought for a moment. "Otherwise you'll become seriously depressed.

"Everyone needs emotional sustenance, whether they're healthy or sick. I have clients who are healthy and have plenty of money but they're practically suicidal. They feel their lives have no meaning. They need emotional sustenance. But with chronic illness, you need it more."

What experiences inspired and transformed me? she asked. Listening to music? Being in the company of certain people? Were there biographies that spoke to the dilemmas I faced? Some ideas instantly sprang to my mind. I had always felt uplifted by Gregorian chants and liturgical music; being in the mountains or feeling close to nature; reading about wise, courageous people who had transcended adversity, who were fully alive; creating things like a wild, artistic cake; and being with certain friends.

After the therapy session, I drove over to the library. That day, I began devouring stories about inspiring people who had made their lives a kind of triumph despite terrible adversity. I read not only for inspiration but also to discover who I might become. A documentary about Nelson Mandela, president of South Africa, became a favorite; history will probably see him as one of the most extraordinary people of our time. Ironically, he may not have been such an extraordinary or deep person had he not endured extraordinary tragedy and suffering. Mandela went into prison a strong man, but he came out powerful.

Biographies of political prisoners particularly resonated with me because of how these people were shut away in jail for years and punished for speaking their minds. My breakfasts were moved to the living room, where I could begin the day looking out at distant evergreen trees while listening to liturgical music. A month later, it amazed me to discover how much these simple efforts had lifted my spirits. Cultivating this steady diet of inspiration was clearly a habit worth keeping, even if my health did return.

With time, other ideas emerged for improving the quality of my days. In nice weather, lunch could be transformed into a picnic by the lake. Rainy days brought out my passion for sewing, although I could now only do small bits of it before it aggravated my arthritis. I noticed that my spirits improved if I was laughing or learning, so most days included a half-hour of a funny movie or television show like "MASH" re-runs. When I stumbled on Book TV, a show that broadcast author readings of nonfiction books from all over the country, I could be learning as I heard lectures on a wide variety of topics. Or I might educate myself by watching a travel or cooking show.

Sometimes my efforts to improve my life were as simple as calling a friend while lying on the couch. Before bedtime, writing down details of the day that I appreciated or that had brought me joy helped me focus on what was going well. On the worst days, when nothing came to mind, there was always "grateful that I live in a free country" or "having a roof over my head" or "grateful I'm not cracking up!" Mark Twain's quote "I have spent most of my life worrying about things that have never happened" sat propped on the windowsill above the kitchen sink to remind me of the futility of worrying about how my life would turn out.

Using my imagination seemed all the more important in transforming my illness experience. Instead of only seeing what was before me, my imagination helped me put things together in a new way. It helped me to be able to pull rabbits out of a hat on even my darkest days. When forced to spend a lot of time watching television, I invented an Audrey Hepburn film festival and watched a string of the actress' movies.

Or after I realized I was not going to have children of my own, out of grief I got creative and started the Fluffernutter Club by asking two neighborhood children if they'd like to join. Club meetings always included a creative project, like baking and decorating ladybug cupcakes for the local firefighters. Sometimes, if the children's stuffed animals had been on their best behavior, we'd throw a birthday party for them. The storybook character Mrs. Piggle-Wiggle usually left us a treasure hunt, although we never got to actually see her. Afterward, we always had a tea party with fluffernutter sandwiches made of peanut butter and marshmallow fluff. In the summer we put on a circus at my neighborhood's annual barbecue and invited the rest of the children in the neighborhood to join the production along with their pets. Sometimes we camped out in my yard.

During my sickest years, I would have to pick up the children's clothes beforehand and wash them with my unscented laundry soap so their outfits wouldn't make me sick. Today I don't need to go to such lengths, although club meetings still wear me out and I must schedule time to recover afterward.

I have been running the club for 11 years now and have added other club members who come to my home two to three kids at a time. The oldest ones are now 14 years old, but since I've adapted activities as they age, they show no signs of outgrowing it. I even introduce club mottos for the older kids from time to time, such as "The best things in life aren't things" and give them one-on-one cooking classes. We have some serious fun together and, while it's not the same as having children of my own, I've concluded that for me it's equally marvelous, just in a different way. Given the demands of my illness, it's all worked out very well in the end.

Gradually the thought dawned on me that there was something more important than healing going on. I came to see that how I coped with the struggle, and the person I became because of the struggle, was going to be a bigger accomplishment than getting healthy. I didn't work any less at getting better. But physical healing became the second priority.

Meanwhile, my health was improving even if progress was painfully slow. If recovery had taken only a year, my new habits for healthful living might have slipped back into oblivion. But partly because it took so long, the changes I'd made became just another way of living. In some ways, the adjustments that had been forced on me had fostered a better quality of life. Having to spend more time outdoors, eat wholesome foods, air out my house by bringing the outside in, and create sources of emotional sustenance made me feel the profound joy of feeling a part of nature. This joy was different from the kind of joy I had experienced before. It brought a sense of peace. And though I wasn't housebound by choice, being so made my life feel more centered.

❧

Increasingly, my chemical illness seemed like a metaphor for modern life estranged from nature. People used to live by the rhythm of the natural world. The only food they could get was organic and their products were free of chemical fragrances; the air was cleaner and they spent more time outside. Today we live in round-the-clock activity, traveling the globe while sending e-mails and talking on cellular telephones. In keeping up with our conveniences, we increasingly try to live at the pace of machines. We're growing more impatient, and homes have become more like refueling stations. What we call progress has encouraged us to try to do it all and have it all – at expense to the soul.

Although technology has changed our pace and way of living, our needs haven't changed much. Some of the most meaningful experiences still come from walks in the woods, or being in the company of family and friends. Instinctive, gut feelings and spiritual experiences continue to produce many of our finest thoughts. We cannot turn back time, nor would we want to. It all boils down to balance, to nourishing and staying in touch with our essence.

With all the changes illness brought, I was surprised to find myself now growing healthier in body, mind and soul than I had been before. Basing the definition of health solely on the state of my body now seemed a limited view. Still, with all the new strains on my life and the people around me, I often wondered how everything was going to turn out.

PART II

DIAGNOSIS

Listening to the Experts

They usually arrived on Saturdays out of the blue. The letters from the District would begin, "Dear Ms. Lipscomb," although they were written by a District colleague I had been on a first-name basis with for five years. The District had ordered another independent medical exam because officials there claimed they needed more opinions to assess my case. These letters never mentioned the specific purpose of the appointment, or the doctor's specialty. They just decreed Thou shalt attend. Each one-to-two-hour exam cost the District up to $1,500.

The independent medical exams, or IMEs, were always scheduled without consulting me, and often with only two weeks' notice. Each one took three to four hours, including time commuting and filling out forms. If I had a prior commitment, I was expected to cancel it. The letters always ended with a threat to stop paying me benefits if I didn't show up. What benefits, I would wonder? At this point, the District was not paying me anything. Once my own three months of sick leave and donated leave from other staff had run out, I'd stopped receiving my salary, and I had to pay my monthly health insurance premium.

When I received such mail, I would say to Ted, "more claptrap from the planet of bureaucratic rigmarole!" He would just groan and roll his eyes. Nothing had prepared me for how excruciating the "evaluation" process would be, especially how hard it would be on my already shipwrecked health. These letters would plunge me into anguish for days. How many exams were needed to come to a conclusion about whether my injuries were work-related? Why didn't L&I stand up to the District and stop this charade? Didn't my three attempts to work in the building, each time resulting in more severe illness, count for anything? But in the end, in order to preserve my chance of receiving compensation, I had no choice but to comply.

Over the years the District would have me examined by a parade of neurologists, occupational medicine doctors, hearing specialists, and psychiatrists. The mental exams were particularly trying. "Do you enjoy sex?" the psychiatrists would ask. "Describe your dreams. Have you ever thought of killing yourself?"

Nearly a year after becoming ill, my claim went to the Washington Department of Labor & Industry's new Chemical Related Illnesses Unit. This department, modeled after the department's Asbestos Unit, had opened in response to pressure from the state Legislature, which was receiving complaints from chemically ill workers about having their claims denied. Since the District had contested my claim, the CRI Unit would make the final decision. Three parties were now involved in my claim: the District, L&I, and Morgan Thomas.

Some days this triangle felt like a bizarre three-ring circus. I often couldn't tell who was in charge, or even whom I should call with questions. Sometimes the purpose behind the IMEs was anybody's guess. For instance, I was sent to three hearing exams to evaluate my ringing ears, even though the first two found my hearing perfectly normal. Each organization I questioned about the need for more hearing exams would direct me to call one of the others. You have the wrong department, each one inevitably told me. Clearly, this runaround could go on indefinitely. The Catch-22 was that if I got angry during a bureaucratic wrangle, the bureaucrats grew cool and talked to me as if I were a hysterical woman.

When my symptoms continued after I had left the District building, skepticism mounted. Perhaps I wanted to get out of working, one of the doctors suggested. Maybe I hadn't gotten over my father's death, theorized another. My father had died of cancer seven years earlier. Pseudo-scientific labels were tossed around: somatoform disorder (or hypochondria), psychological conditioning, histrionic personality, all of which implied that my physical symptoms were psychological.

Most of the IMEs went something like the one with Drs. Ewing and Roadcap. Arriving at their office on a spring afternoon, I checked in with a receptionist who sat in a self-standing cubicle in an otherwise empty room, like a lonely tent thrown up in a barren desert. The office had a just-moved-in feeling about it. In fact, the two physicians were part of a company whose sole purpose was to perform IMEs for employers, insurance companies and disability programs. Since the employers paid the bills, they were the consumers who needed to be satisfied, not the patients. Unlike other medical settings, here no one cared if you got well. That wasn't their department. The doctors' only job was to evaluate whether my condition was "more-probably-than-not" caused by my workplace – defined as a greater than 50 percent chance.

Handing me pages of paperwork to fill out, the receptionist motioned for me to sit down in the waiting area across the way. At the top of the first page: *Please describe your injury. Show us* [on a diagram of a human body] *where you have pain.* A woman next to me nervously flipped through magazines. Another man hopped about on crutches. Suddenly a woman appeared before me. "Miss Lipscomb? We're ready for you." She led me into an examining room where a woman was spraying air freshener.

"Just freshening up after the last patient!" the woman cheerfully exclaimed, flitting about like a crop-dusting plane. An overpowering, sweet smell stung my nose, hitting me wave after wave like the blow of a hammer. I coughed and began to feel nauseated. Abruptly, the same woman came back and told me to move to another examining room. There she began spraying more air freshener about. I wanted to ask her to stop, but feared being labeled paranoid. By the time the doctors arrived, my insides quivered like a bowl full of gelatin.

Dr. Ewing was a slight man with a chiseled, purposeful face. He extended his hand, looking at the wall behind me, as if he couldn't wait to be done with me. I may as well have been someone's family pet who had wandered into the place. He motioned vaguely toward a chair against the wall. I guessed that he meant for me to sit down. About 10 feet away, across an empty room, both doctors sat behind a long, narrow table. If they had wanted to intimidate claimants, this setup would have done the trick. I felt like I was in a courtroom with two judges presiding from on high.

"First, do you have any questions?" Dr. Ewing asked.

"Yes," I replied. "I know that MCS is not a well-established diagnosis. But do you favor any theory about what causes it?"

Dr. Ewing rambled on incoherently, evading my question. My hair stood up on the back of my neck. Not a good sign, I thought. My hopes for a fair trial evaporated quickly. His reply made me suspect he might have a built-in bias against the condition.

For the next two hours, the doctors questioned and examined me. They didn't find anything unusual that would explain the cause of my health troubles. Next came a personal history. "Where did you go to college?" Dr. Ewing asked.

"Princeton University."

The doctor arched his eyebrows, clearly surprised. "Really?" he said. "How long have you been married?"

"Nine years."

"Hmmmm," he murmured. As Ewing questioned me, Dr. Roadcap proceeded to check my reflexes and look into my ears like a mechanic working on a car. A heavyset man wearing thick, gold jewelry, Dr. Sollek reeked of cologne, which made me gag.

"How long have you been at the District?" Dr. Roadcap asked.

"Nine years."

"Really!?" Again, the raised eyebrows poised in near disbelief.

"How long have you been in your house?"

"Five years."

When they asked where I grew up, I told them about my childhood in Africa and extensive travels. The doctor looked taken aback. I began to wonder if I wasn't fitting their notions about the type of person who got MCS. I was also getting the same response in my other independent medical exams. It was as if the doctors had me stereotyped as a not-too-bright hysterical person who was afraid of getting out in the world.

With the exam nearly completed, Dr. Ewing asked me if I wanted to add anything. "Yes," I answered. "I think you should know that at least 60 other people in my office building have similar health symptoms. I've typed up a one-page list of facts about these illnesses. All of them can be verified." I began to cross the room.

Dr. Roadcap appeared unnerved, as if leaving my station was a menacing act. "That's not part of our job!" Dr. Ewing exclaimed, swiftly and surely. "We're only supposed to answer the questions we were given."

"Couldn't you suggest that someone examine the building further and question other employees to help prevent other workers from getting sick and to see if there are similarities between our symptoms?"

He shook his head like a determined bulldog. "That's not our department." Here we go again, I thought. Taking action never seems to fall under anyone's department.

Weeks later, the doctors mailed their eight-page report to the District. Drs. Ewing and Roadcap concluded that my symptoms existed before I moved to the new office, and that "almost certainly" they resulted from psychological problems. They neglected to mention that other employees might have symptoms similar to mine. "We believe," they wrote, "that she is so conditioned to responding to even thinking about the Puget Sound Trade District, that she will develop subjective symptoms if asked to go back there."

Further down the page, they referred to my pre-existing arthritis symptoms to imply that I had secretly been a hypochondriac all along. Perhaps, they briefly acknowledged, I had been physically affected the first few months in the building by low-level irritants; but by now the problem would certainly be psychological, as if by some magical expectation, I should have gotten better. They gave no evidence to support their conclusion. I was expected to provide overwhelming, indisputable scientific evidence linking my illness to the workplace, but they did not hold themselves to the same standard when they offered armchair psychologizing, hardly an empirical procedure.

Some facts they even didn't get straight. "She only worked in the building five weeks." (In addition to the first five weeks, I worked for more than two months in the building during attempt No. 3 to continue with my job.) "She has previously been evaluated for anxiety." (I had not.) "Today's exam doesn't reveal any evidence of arthritis." (They didn't perform an arthritis evaluation.) "She has a history of vomiting." (I hadn't thrown up since having the flu more than 20 years earlier.) "She is very focused on her body." (I wondered how they could determine this in an exam specifically held to discuss my body.) And my favorite sentence: "Her age is 43, and she appears younger than her stated age." (Maybe that's because I was 37.)

Most of the other IMEs continued in the same vein. The examiners had a special gift for finding the evidence they had already decided must be there; and they could twist their reports and manipulate their findings. Even when my psychological tests turned out normal, one psychiatrist said the exam was of no use because I had tried to deny my psychological problems.

My experience with the IMEs reminded me of several research experiments that document how health professionals often diagnose normal behavior as pathological. In one experiment, eight mentally healthy people were placed in a psychiatric hospital and told to behave in their usual manner. None of the hospital doctors discovered they were fakes, although some of the other patients realized it. Instead, the doctors labeled the participants' behavior as sick. For instance, one "patient" who took notes during the experiment was diagnosed as engaging in pathological "writing behavior," though no one ever looked at his notes.

In another experiment, a group of psychologists listened to a tape they were told was a recording of a counseling session. But the tape really featured an actor playing the role of a relaxed, confident man who didn't have any psychological problems. Nevertheless, 43 percent of the therapists diagnosed him as psychotic or neurotic and 19 percent said he had adjustment problems. The more IMEs I went to, the more I felt I was trapped in the same place as the people in these studies.

I tried to fight back and get false information about me corrected in the IME reports, but my objections were ignored and disappeared into a black hole. In any event, doing so involved a Catch-22: Trying to set the record straight made me look defensive, as if I had something to hide. I began to sympathize with celebrities who find themselves the subject of false stories written by tabloid reporters who want to sell as many newspapers as possible.

Despite my best efforts to stop the exams, they dragged on for two-and-a-half years. The more IMEs I went to, the thicker my chart got. The bigger my chart grew, the more I was perceived as a hypochondriac. And since each doctor built on the previous doctor's skewed evidence, the painted picture of me grew increasingly distorted over time. During what ended up being my last IME, the doctor concluded that my fear of chemicals was so overblown, he didn't think me capable of returning to any kind of work ever again.

"These exams are beginning to remind me of the children's game Telephone," my primary care physician said one day. "One doctor says something, and the next one repeats what he thinks the last doctor said. It's taken on a life of its own." Amazed, Dr. Osborne shook her head sadly.

Although she was asked to comment on the findings of each IME, whatever Dr. Osborne said was ignored; anything the medical examiners said stuck. During more than 10 years of knowing me, Dr. Osborne wrote to the District that she had never known me to be a hypochondriac. While the specific cause of MCS was controversial, my symptoms certainly seemed to fit the scientific model of cause and effect. To make the process fair, she suggested, doctors with a middle-of-the-road orientation should examine me. But, like mine, her words were carried off by the hot bureaucratic wind.

For a time, I decided to give the IME doctors the benefit of the doubt. Perhaps their stereotypes of me as a hysterical, unintelligent woman came from not knowing me. Maybe I should tell them more about myself. So when asked where I went to college and high school in two IMEs, I volunteered my academic ranking. After all, that was "objective" information, served up the way they liked it. But my plan backfired: One physician used that statement to label me an overachiever. Another wrote, "Despite her accomplishments, there appears to be some feeling of inadequacy." What a difference it would have made to my spirits if the IME physicians could have been humble and admitted they didn't know enough about what ailed me, that medicine didn't have all the answers.

Eventually, I had to develop strategies to deal with the Catch-22 of the exams. When a friend suggested consulting a psychologist to evaluate whether stress or emotions might have caused my health problems, I decided to give it a try. Five appointments and four psychological tests later, all at my expense, psychologist Dr. Elliott Humphrey said he could find no evidence of psychosomatic problems. If I had become psychologically conditioned to odors, he explained, the test results would have turned out differently. Despite Dr. Humphrey's conclusion, the District extrapolated a sentence from his report and saw it as evidence that I needed yet another psychiatric exam.

Fortunately, in the end, I had not consulted Dr. Humphrey in vain. Seeing that the help I needed was dealing with the workers' compensation system, he referred me to Adeline Crinks, an advocate for injured workers, who owned a company called On the Job Injuries. When I first met Adeline, an enormous weight was lifted from my shoulders. Smart, tough and well-respected, Adeline was referred to at Labor & Industries as the Dragon Lady. A spunky, athletic blonde, Adeline expressed surprise that my claim hadn't been accepted. She pointed out that between the doctors I had consulted on my own and the District's first IMEs, seven doctors had said I had MCS, on a more probable than not basis, and that it originated from my workplace.

"What is the problem?" she exclaimed. Her melodious Scottish accent poured over me like a soothing balm. I shrugged, relaxing into the chair. One by one, Adeline read my IME reports, growing more indignant with each one. "What are you wearing to the exams?" she asked, looking up.

"A pair of pants and a shirt. I've purposely dressed plainly so the doctors won't say I look too well to be sick."

"Oh no," Adeline said, shaking her head emphatically, "wear a skirt and jewelry. Put on makeup." She shifted in her chair. "They're more likely to say you're coping well." Surprised by her suggestion, I remembered a psychiatrist's report that described me as "neatly dressed and noted to be wearing very little makeup or jewelry."

"Do you have a short skirt?" Adeline asked, glancing at my legs. I threw my head back and roared, nearly choking with laughter. "If you have one, wear it," she continued, looking up from my chart. "They've been known to be influenced by a pair of good legs." This woman was a breath of fresh air, a life preserver thrown to me in these turbulent seas.

So for my next exam, I dressed to the nines. Jewelry, makeup, a black skirt and amethyst silk blouse. My friend Christina Flournoy, who was visiting from the East Coast and who would wait in the reception area during the appointment, volunteered to dress up, too, in case her appearance should reflect upon me. There we were getting ready for the exam, in a flurry of trying on skirts and choosing earrings as if dressing for a date. When Christina ran into my bedroom asking, "How do I look?" as she spread out her arms and twirled around, I laughed at the absurd turn my life had taken. It turned out Adeline was right. Once I began dressing up for the exams, no doctor again would say I looked depressed.

Adeline helped me better understand the workers' compensation system as well. The IME doctors, she explained, usually function like defense physicians in a lawsuit, meaning that since the District paid the bills for the exams, the doctors were more likely to give an opinion the District wanted to hear – that my health problems had nothing to do with their building. It comes down to the almighty dollar, she said. Employers pay a huge amount of money for workers' compensation, so they would rather fight injured workers in order to keep their costs down.

In many instances the IME doctors are retired and they haven't had updated training or education in 10 to 15 years so they're not up-to-date on the latest medical information. They make good money doing IMEs – some make a quarter of a million dollars a year from the exams – and they do not have the expense of carrying malpractice insurance or maintaining offices. Most of the time, Adeline pointed out, injured workers have no idea how the system works and they'll do everything their employer tells them to do, without knowing when their claim isn't being handled correctly. Then if the claim is denied, the injured worker doesn't know what to do about it.

Originally, the workers' compensation system wasn't intended to be so adversarial; it was set up as a simple no-fault system. But the mere fact that she had been doing this advocacy work for 14 years would confirm that these claims are often not handled appropriately and benefits are denied to workers who have been injured on the job, she told me.

During these years, Labor & Industries, which oversaw the District's program, cut businesses' workers' compensation insurance premiums by an average of 10 percent. It was able to do so, it boasted, without denying anyone benefits. I also learned what an effective job insurance companies and businesses have done to cultivate public sympathy. Educated and usually sophisticated friends and acquaintances often rationalized the District's behavior by saying it had to protect itself from cheaters. Hardly ever did anyone mention that employers routinely deny benefits, and define health problems narrowly, to keep costs down and maximize profits. Somehow, thanks to businesses' effective public relations campaigns, we've gotten this skewed notion that the majority of people cheat, when, in fact, most are honest. By the insurance industry's own estimates, roughly 10 percent of claims are fraudulent. That means 90 percent of them are legitimate.

Several doctors and a friend who previously had worked for IME companies shared their experiences with me, and they reinforced Adeline's observations. One doctor told me he had stopped doing the exams because of the pressure to rule against the workers. Another doctor explained why he chose to do the exams. "After you've watched enough of your patients treated unfairly in IMEs," Dr. Rick Noble said, "you either decide to stand at the edge and criticize the system, or to become part of it and offer an independent voice. I chose to do the latter, and signed up with several IME companies."

"How do they work?" I asked.

"The doctors are well-paid for the exams, and they don't risk much of a chance of malpractice suits because of the way they're set up," he said. "Almost all of the physicians who do them are under financial pressure. Usually they're starting up a medical practice, or they're retired, or healthcare reform has made their practice unstable. The problem is that if a physician gives an opinion an employer or insurance company doesn't want to hear more than two or three times, he's not asked back. So there's a continuous weeding-out process going on."

I guess I should not have been surprised, I thought, sinking further into my chair, as if pushed down by a heavy weight. I found it hard to believe this system has such a seal of authority.

Dr. Nobel explained the plight of a patient in an IME: "The patient is guilty until proven innocent. Even if you present evidence that you can't work right now, the doctor will often decide it's not enough proof. And how can you give enough proof when your health problem isn't extremely obvious? The answer is, you can't. Maybe, just maybe, an examiner will accept what you say if you are seriously disfigured, or if you've lost both legs and can't speak."

I began to laugh but stopped abruptly when I saw that Dr. Noble's expression remained solemn. He was serious.

"For a panel exam – that is an evaluation by several physicians – doctors are invited to arrive an hour early. They go through your chart together, and whether or not they realize it, they form an opinion about you before you even walk through that door. Generally, most of them scoff at your evidence. Even if there is an impartial doctor in the room, there are usually enough scoffers to poison the atmosphere."

Whether or not they admit it, the businesses and agencies ordering the IMEs are as much a party to this system as the medical examiners. Everyone who participates bears some responsibility. Before hiring Adeline, I had searched in vain for legal help. No lawyers experienced with chemical illnesses would take my case. One lawyer told me: "The employers fight these chemical injury claims with a vengeance. It's too difficult and expensive to prove you've been harmed. I'm sorry, but I'm not taking these cases anymore. I'm just not winning them."

Some useful advice for coping with my circumstances came from Sherry Pierce. Well-experienced with the workers' compensation system because of a back injury, Sherry was someone I occasionally called for help. One day I complained to her that the District had requested files from a therapist I had consulted. In order to be considered for workers' compensation, I had had to sign a form that gave my employer unlimited access to any files and other information about me that they claimed would help them evaluate my claim. How could the District, I asked Sherry, do this when I hadn't been diagnosed with mental problems?

Would it help if the therapist wrote a letter saying I was psychologically healthy?

"Anne," Sherry burst out in frustration, "you've got to stop laboring under the delusion that they'll listen if you give them more information. When will you get it? Understanding isn't the point! The more files they get into, the more they'll want. The more information they have, the more there is to manipulate. It will go on and on."

I was stunned. But that moment set me free. Finally I realized what the problem was: I was taking the bureaucrats at their word. *We need more information to evaluate your claim.* The insight brought a wave of relief. Accepting the way things really were would give me so much more time and energy for healing.

❧

As the saga wore on, my greatest challenge remained dealing with all of the anger. I had to cultivate ways to defuse it. Finding humor in ordinary situations proved to be the best way. It wasn't hard to do. As the situation unfolded, it got funnier. Bureaucrats and medical examiners began to seem like fops in a surrealist novel. The lengths to which they went to discredit me became absurd.

Joan and I shared a kind of private gallows humor. Ted always knew when we were talking on the telephone because I would be laughing so hard. We invented mottoes for everyone: The advertising slogan for the District's Facilities Department became "Buildings before people"; for the Morgan Thomas insurance company, "It's a good idea to offer disability benefits, but a disgrace if you have to use them!"; for the Department of Labor & Industries, "The wheels of progress grind slowly." The overall theme for the saga was, "You have the wrong department." And Joan would attach little notes to information she mailed me, "Like sands in the hourglass ... so go the days of our lives – As the District Turns, Part LXIX."

A visualizing technique helped me deal with the worst of my anger. I would picture myself walking into the examining room swinging a baseball bat over my head; then I proceeded to knock some sense into the insurance doctor. Or I imagined myself a hulking giant with insect-sized bureaucrats and doctors crawling on my skin. I would shake them off and walk away. Sometimes I simply punched pillows. These simple techniques helped dissipate my anger, allowing me to focus on other more important matters, like my health.

Sometimes when District letters arrived, I would ask Ted to read them to me first. Hearing the news of another scheduled IME through Ted somehow softened the blow. After getting used to the idea, I would read the letter myself. Ted always felt angry and helpless watching me deal with the situation. One day, before an impending exam, we walked along Lake Washington, where the luminous water was dappled with sailboats anchoring an aquamarine sky. The day was impossibly beautiful and made me feel that I lived in a resort. A row of poplar trees cast their long, narrow shadows across the golden lawn. In the distance, seagulls squeaked a celebratory song. I never tired of the quality of blue light in Seattle, the kind of light that brought out the full depth of nature's colors. In Egypt, we had enjoyed sun day after day, but its bright glare had often bleached out the landscape, making it a paler version of itself. I slipped my arm through Ted's.

"Do you want me to go to the exam with you?" Ted asked, burying his hands in his pockets. "It's hard for me to get time off from work, but I'll go if it would help you."

The roar of a hydroplane about to land upon the glittering lake disrupted our conversation. "Thanks, but I'll be all right," I said, touched that he would offer. Just having him extend his support gave me a lift. "You'd think I would be getting numb to them by now."

We walked together in an affectionate silence. An unusual sight caught my eye. A man on a skateboard sailed by, pulled by his galloping golden retriever on a leash. We laughed until they became one small dot on the horizon.

"Ted, what would you think if I gave up fighting the workers' compensation claim? I don't know how much more I can take," I said in a quivering voice, fighting back hot tears. "Fighting an ugly battle while I'm sick is really taking a toll on me. Besides, I have little chance of winning."

"Oh, no," Ted said, his jaw set like a bulldog. "No way. We've lost over half of our income, and they should pay."

"But you're not the one who has to fight the battle," I said, not surprised by his response. I paused in thought. "All right, I'll do my best but oh what a struggle it's turning out to be. I haven't had as much fun since the last time I cleaned the basement!" We turned around and headed back toward the car.

"Anne, I wish you would go with me on my next family vacation," Ted said. "I'm getting tired of going alone when everyone else comes with their partners and children."

"But you know traveling is difficult for me, especially being in a house with that many people."

"I don't see why you can't go," Ted said, frustrated. "It's only once a year."

"The problem is that if I'm lucky, I can handle one trip a year. So if I go with you every year, that would be all I could do. When would the two of us get away? What about seeing my family? What about your family coming out here?" A tense discussion followed. I agreed to go on Ted's family vacations every other year.

ೲ

At District publication manager Joan Bell's house the family had shifted into its fall schedule, the busiest time of the year. Outside of her work at the District, Joan shuttled her children to football and soccer practice and worked on their school carnival and other fundraisers. It was the time of year when Joan would make her rounds at the District's Communications Department to see if anyone wanted to buy magazine subscriptions to support her children's school. Saturdays were devoted to Joan's children's sports games. Joan would head toward one game, her husband to another. One crisp fall day, Joan sat in bleachers at Lincoln play field cheering for the Eagles. Squinting in the sun, she watched her son running headlong down the field. The boys yelled out to each other to pass the ball, and parents added to the noisy chorus.

After the game, Joan called to tell me her MCS had come back that week. "Anne, get ready for another chapter of the saga," Joan said in a voice wearied and downtrodden. I sat down, feeling a heaviness settle about me. "Tuesday I started feeling sick at work. Headaches, ringing in my ears, nausea. Here we go again, I thought. So I looked around and discovered a man using a solvent to remove a stain on the steps next to our department. Right away, I called the building manager to suggest that they notify me when anyone will be using chemicals near my office. After several days at home, the symptoms went away – for now, anyway. The first day, I couldn't do anything. Then I worked from home."

"Joan, did you have your IME with the psychiatrist?"

She groaned. "What a system. Even though I went on at length about the other sick people in the building, about how most people are too frightened to speak up, not a peep of it showed up in the psychiatrist's report to the District. But," she said brightly, "he did write that I mentioned my husband is overweight. Now that's relevant!" We roared with laughter.

Eventually, thanks to the moveable slats that were installed on the vents in Joan's office, her symptoms disappeared. Joan thought her health troubles and the IMEs were finally behind her when an employee called one day from the department that managed the workers' compensation program. The District wanted to send Joan to more independent medical exams, she said. But why, she wondered? My health problems have gone away. Because we're sending Anne Lipscomb to more exams and we want to make your cases equitable. It was too late, Joan replied, too late for that! Joan felt relieved when the effort was dropped.

When all was said and done, my personal doctor's counsel proved to be most prescient, even though Dr. Osborne had much less experience with chemical illnesses than some of the specialists to whom the District sent me. Indeed, if I had listened to her early on when she advised getting another job, I might have contained the damage to my health. Instead, wanting to believe the specialists who told me everything would be all right, and upset about losing work I enjoyed, and buying into the illusion that my condition couldn't be serious if it wasn't documented on tests, I chose to disregard her advice and my body's warning signals. Had I known how bad this condition could get, I would have taken action more quickly.

Finding the Energy Within

The first eight months of my illness, I had dragged myself around, simply trying to hold my life together. It was as if foreign troops had moved into my body on that first day in the new office and their arrival had turned into a long, drawn-out occupation. Nights offered no relief, as my usual deep sleep had turned into a light dozing punctuated by wide-awake hours wincing in pain that coursed through my chest, head and stomach. I despaired at a life lived solely at the level of coping with my body. Not knowing what was going on, or when the situation would end, seemed unbearable at times. Not even a year before, life had not been like this. Let this be a temporary nightmare, I would silently plead. Let one of the doctors or air quality experts come up with *the* solution.

In the beginning, worries pressed upon me: Would these health problems be permanent? Would I ever know again what it was to run down the street, or to go anywhere without first calculating what my body could handle? How could I live without being a productive member of society? Part of this pressure came from thinking about how others would perceive me. I must confess I wasted time worrying about what other people must have thought of me and my newfound predicament since some seemed to wonder if the problems weren't all in my head.

Our society highly values *doing*. You simply cannot escape this. When someone asks, "How have you been?" we'll often say, "Keeping busy!" as if that is a desirable state. We often equate being busy with having an important, interesting life. But activity can be a drug just the same, and we're always looking for the next fix. Adding to the pressure, an unspoken belief in our culture often conveys to us that if we're not employed, we're a nobody.

Not all cultures place such a premium on action and money. For instance, where Americans tend to love *doing*, the French particularly admire *thinking*. When intellectuals die in France, their obituaries regularly make the front page of newspapers. I've always found it interesting that dinner parties with friends in France are more likely to include a lively exchange of opinions about politics, art, or religion. At social gatherings in the United States, we're more apt to discuss what we've been *doing*, and part of our identity comes from what we do for a living. In France, who you are and what you think about things are often more important than what you do for work. You may spend a long evening with people at a dinner party and return home not knowing what any of them does for a living.

Gradually, though, how others perceived me in this way started to seem irrelevant. It became increasingly clear that the core of me wasn't about what I did or whether I was making money. My value came from who I was as a person and the ways I could contribute to the well being of others within my limitations. Until my medical leave, I had known this intellectually; now I really believed it, or rather came to live it. And the shift was liberating. With time, the thought of seeing myself as only existing through activity or money seemed absurd.

Eventually other truths emerged that reason could not touch. It surprised me, for instance, to discover that the more open and accepting I became of my pain, the more I could let myself grieve over my losses, the happier I felt, the stronger I grew, the freer my mind became. Instead of wasting energy on trying to avoid pain, I could use it to grow. Within all of the apparent contradictions, I found some unexpected truths.

The first year of my illness demonstrated that resting and avoiding chemicals would not be enough to help me heal. Doing nothing was getting me nowhere. Also, I clearly had to get away from pessimistic doctors who thought recovering from MCS was practically hopeless or that it was a psychological condition. They were not only too negative, but their advice – about returning to the building and pretending this wasn't serious – had further damaged my health. And so I embarked on a personal quest for recovery.

Having seen how little was known about chemical-related illnesses, even among the physicians and air quality experts who had some experience with it, I instinctively felt I had to step up to the plate and take responsibility for coming up with a healthcare plan. The task seemed practically overwhelming, but being passive seemed worse. At this point I still harbored hopes I might find a kind of magic bullet, like a healthcare provider or remedy that would cure the problem. I didn't fully grasp what I was up against, nor did I have any idea that my quest to heal would expand beyond my body into a personal and spiritual journey of its own.

At the time, reviewing my life felt like sizing up the kitchen after a pressure cooker had exploded all over it. Poring over books and talking to other chemically ill people was a messy and confusing process, but a list of potential healthcare providers and treatments eventually emerged. Most people who had experienced at least a partial recovery reported that the process took them between four and 11 years. Healing was slow because they couldn't totally avoid the things that made them sick. After all, they couldn't stop breathing the air. Hearing this unwelcome news would make me sigh and wonder if I was up to the task. Who knew whether the therapies would help me in the end?

Since mainstream physicians weren't treating this condition, most people recommended alternative healthcare practitioners. Living on the West Coast offered many options. I began to consult one practitioner after another, trying their suggestions to see what might help. Keeping a careful daily record of my symptoms and their severity helped me figure out what worked. This process could be murky, but patterns surfaced over time.

IME doctors scoffed at my resorting to alternative care, and some friends questioned whether the effort was worth it. I had some doubts myself but decided to suspend my disbelief. To refrain from trying therapies meant I might as well announce, fine, let my life be a shambles. Meanwhile life was slipping by. I couldn't sit by without trying.

When I evaluated various healthcare systems, two criteria proved to be particularly important: How much experience did the practitioner have treating environmental illness? And how well did the therapies work for my individual body? Because the fact that a health therapy had worked on other chemically ill people did not necessarily mean it would help me. Aggressive therapies didn't work for me at all. For example, instead of following a specific detoxification plan in the beginning to get chemicals out, such as saunas or homeopathic food powders, I had to rely on exercise and drinking lots of water to do the job more slowly.

☙

Acupuncture's gentle approach proved to be one my body could tolerate. Eastern medicine doesn't generally treat specific symptoms and diseases, as traditional Western medicine does. Instead it tends to seek overall balance and strength for the body. The first time I met Joe Metcalf, an acupuncturist practicing traditional Chinese medicine, who also had experience with chemical illnesses, he said my body energy was extremely weak. "You are a very sick young woman," Joe concluded, shaking his head.

Chinese medicine believes that patterns of energy, or *chi*, run through the body. I remembered once seeing a poster of those energy channels mapped onto a human body. They looked like a system of highways and roads to all parts of the body. When this vital energy moves freely and is balanced, Chinese medicine believes it creates an inhospitable environment for intruders. In acupuncture, an imbalance in *chi* is seen as the cause of sickness; the *chi* may be blocked, too weak, or too strong. To help restore harmony and health, an acupuncturist inserts needles the width of a human hair into the body at specific points, thereby manipulating energy flows.

"Stick out your tongue," Joe said. "Its color and the coating on it will help show me your imbalances." He took my pulse at several places on my wrist. My eye fell on the table beside him, its surface covered with small bottles labeled in Chinese. Assorted glass jars held packets of needles, clusters of cotton balls, and rubbing alcohol. What looked something like a cigar lay perched in a metal cup. A self-standing heater provided extra warmth in this softly lit room, to help patients' *chi* flow better.

"Anne, you have a yin deficiency," Joe explained. "The yin is the restorative aspect of the energy; it's the resting phase, like the repolarizing of the heart muscle so that it can fire again."

"What does that mean?"

"When you exercise and get really sore afterward," Joe replied, "a yin deficiency keeps you from getting deep sleep, so the restorative parts of your body can't function. You'll wake up sore the next morning, and it will take a long time for the pain to disappear." He pulled down my lower eyelid and looked into my eyes. "You also have a spleen disorder. In Chinese medicine, the spleen is the major organ of digestion. Your digestion is so compromised that you're probably only getting half of the nutrients from your food."

"Can you help me?" I asked.

"The bottom line is that people's systems are always trying to heal themselves. In acupuncture, we try to jump-start your system. I can't force someone in your condition to become well. I have to augment your system so that you become well. It's the difference between manipulation and nurturing."

"Would my arthritis have caused this *yin* deficiency?"

"No. There is some event that triggers a process this significant."

"Some doctors think my emotions or other stresses caused this."

"Your emotions could not have caused something like this," Joe said firmly.

He then left the room, instructing me to undress and lie face down on the cushioned table. Returning, he placed his hand inches above my back, pausing to feel my energy flow. Joe told me the *chi* felt like movement in a certain direction; the quality of the energy he found during each appointment would determine his treatment that day. He began inserting needles along my spine and in my ankles while explaining that he only had a three-millimeter range to accurately reach each point. In the beginning months, my body could only tolerate two to four needles because my *chi* was so weak. As my energy grew stronger, he could add more needles. It would take me a year to begin feeling the *chi*. The first time, the *chi* felt like a faint tickle, as if a bug was crawling around on the front of my throat, and I wanted to flick it off. Eventually I could sense its subtle currents, like a barely perceptible breeze, moving in a particular direction in my body. What a relief it was to find someone who could go to work on me without wasting time, questioning whether or not my illness was real.

"Do you see similarities among your chemically sensitive patients?" I asked.

"Oh, yes," Joe nodded. "I see the same tendency, but it manifests itself differently in each person's constitution. There are about eight general types of body constitutions. This MCS condition overlaid on my constitution would be a different story. If I were to see people having health problems in the District building, I would probably see a linking thread between them. It would be variations on a theme."

I lay there trying to understand this very different Eastern system of thought. How in the world, I wondered, did people originally develop it thousands of years ago? After all, you couldn't open up a body and see the energy patterns. This was all so different from our Western orientation. Acupuncture was a medicine of correlation.

The fact that Joe could tell so much about my body without ordering tests amazed me. But then I remembered that our society relies heavily on tests and objective information. People who consult general practitioners in the United States receive more tests than in almost any European country. When health problems had cropped up at the Puget Sound Trade District, managers treated numbers and data as more important than employees' experiences. And since the tests didn't reveal any gross problems, peoples' health reactions weren't considered altogether real. In any case, no one seemed to know how to proceed without statistics and numbers. Nevertheless, the problem existed whether or not tests validated it.

During my illness, I noticed that Eastern and alternative healthcare providers valued my personal observations more than many mainstream physicians. The IME doctors had dismissed them as "subjective" and therefore unreliable. One Chinese doctor even told me, "In China we have a saying: The people with chronic conditions, they are the experts." What a far cry from the Western doctors who had treated me as a simpleton when I could only serve up words to describe my illness. In the end, the healthcare practitioners who took my subjective experience seriously were the ones who helped me the most.

I asked Joe about his thoughts on some of the symptoms and worsening conditions of those working in the new building. He said, "When they're getting headaches, their system is showing that it's stressed. When they're getting asthma, their system is being weakened. Those symptoms are occurring because the body has to deal with something that's not right. This process might start with headaches, and then become digestive disorders after eating; then some urgency in bowel movements might develop; next you're having problems making decisions and remembering things. It goes on and on. The useful thing about Chinese medicine is that we can make connections between seemingly unrelated symptoms, all the way from a headache to emotional problems. We can watch them through time and know that you're not making it up. And these patterns can be detected early on in the process, giving us the ability to recognize disease in its earliest, subtlest stages."

Joe left the room again, instructing me to lie still and rest. Spread out like a porcupine with needles sticking up out of me, I thought about how, in the West, we tend to experience disease as if it springs up overnight and that often a disease has to have caused significant damage before Western medicine picks it up. After awhile Joe returned and felt my back to see how my *chi* was responding to the needles.

At the end of the appointment, Joe handed me a diet which he said would help my body restore balance. In Chinese medicine, each food has an energetic quality to it. Foods are defined as *cold, cool, neutral, warm* or *hot*. Until my *chi* grew stronger, he advised emphasizing neutral foods; meals should be warm and well-cooked, eaten at the same time every day, sitting down, and undisturbed by other activities. Glancing down the page, I noticed that many "hot" foods – garlic, ginger, chocolate, mustard – were ones that made me especially sick.

Joe's explanations were arcane to me. All I could do was follow orders and see if they produced results. On one occasion, for example, I was telling Joe how I barely slept the night after his treatment because a feeling like electrical impulses was shooting through me like a wild fireworks show. He explained that this had happened because my body couldn't use all the energy from his treatment that day. He adjusted his approach and the problem went away.

His suggestion to take protein powder was easier to comprehend. One day I told Joe I'd been craving fish with abandon. He explained that protein allows the body to maintain and repair itself; part of my sleeping problems might mean my body couldn't rest at night because it didn't have adequate protein to mend. Sure enough, almost immediately after beginning the powder, I was getting much better sleep. Happy as I was to discover this, I also felt exasperated. Two years after becoming ill, I was still uncovering new layers of problems. I felt like an onion peeling away, layer after layer. And I had no idea if I was anywhere near a center, or if one even existed.

Exposure to Chinese medicine made me wonder whether our culture's health model puts us at another disadvantage for understanding environmental illnesses. In the United States and England, mainstream medicine tends to view disease as an invader that treatment attacks. Non-specific causes of disease like imbalance, poor nutrition, or environmental toxins have not received much attention. With some diseases, though, a less direct route that strengthens the overall body may promote greater health or at least make further losses less likely.

Interestingly, even though the French practice the same medicine as Americans, they believe in building up the *terrain*, or general constitution, to cure and manage disease. Instead of using antibiotics as much as we do, French doctors tend more toward vitamins, homeopathy, and other therapies that help shore up the body's resistance. Once it surprised me when a French doctor prescribed bed rest for my sick friend; in the United States, she more likely would have been advised to take a pill so she could keep going.

In addition to the acupuncturist, an environmental medicine specialist, Dr. William Cunningham, helped me a great deal. Dr. Cunningham was part of a new medical specialty, which was treating health problems like MCS. The medical establishment, however, did not officially support this specialty. Contrary to most mainstream medical practitioners' beliefs, environmental medicine specialists think that even low levels of synthetic chemicals can adversely affect any of the body's organ systems. They like to point out that some accepted medical problems were once believed to be imaginary or psychological until fully understood. For example, we once considered lead and asbestos to be safe. Environmental medicine specialists see our understanding of chemicals' effects on health as being in its infancy, as our knowledge of lead and asbestos once were.

The mainstream medical community has its reasons for being skeptical. In order to acknowledge a disease, physicians require a collection of symptoms and signs that are the same in everyone. People with diabetes, for instance, have similar manifestations of their disease – such as increased thirst and urine production – and they receive the same treatments. The problem with MCS is that symptoms vary widely among patients, and they change from week to week. Given the way physicians define disease, they can't reach consensus on a precise definition of MCS.

Also, our medical system doesn't believe a disease affects more than one or two organ systems. But MCS symptoms typically involve multiple organs. In medicine, the only diagnosis that fits this phenomenon is *hypochondriac*. One doctor explained this further to me. "In medical school," he said, "we like to hear about one or two complaints from a patient – like 'I've got a headache and my ear hurts.' We can deal with that. We're often taught that if a patient comes in with a list of problems, then he is probably a hypochondriac."

Additionally, to acknowledge a disease, the medical community wants first to understand its mechanism. But such precise, singular understanding of environmental illness remains elusive; in reality, many interacting factors may affect this condition. Many MCS symptoms are similar to problems known to be provoked by solvents and pesticides, except that the ailments aren't believed to occur at low levels of them. In short, MCS is simply not conforming to current scientific understanding of disease.

A lack of good scientific studies contributes to the medical community's reluctance to acknowledge MCS. Officially recognizing a disease requires a body of literature, accepted by the medical community, that proves its existence. Some research on MCS exists, but it doesn't constitute hard science. Unfortunately, variables can't be controlled one at a time – the way medicine likes them to be – since people are exposed to many chemicals simultaneously, and each person has a different tolerance for them. Complicating matters, if you were to expose one group of chemically sensitive people to a chemical, for example, and another to a placebo, the latter group might react to ingredients in the placebo. Therefore, meaningful comparisons become difficult to make. And then there is the predicament that bodies appear to adapt to chemical exposure over time – symptoms seem to disappear but physical damage continues nonetheless – similar to the way an irritated throat or cough can go away while the cigarette smoking habit that caused it is still compromising a person's health.

Even if conducting studies on chemical-related illnesses were easy, securing funding for them is not. Government and academic funding for research has dwindled in recent decades, and businesses like to finance research that promises to boost their profits. They are hardly interested in studies that might find fault with their products. One researcher complained that he could easily get funding for a study that attempted to show MCS had psychological causes; but proposing to research physical causes met with resistance. Not surprisingly, industry-funded studies of other work-related conditions have come to negative conclusions – denying a relationship between the workplace and the disease more frequently than research underwritten through other means.

Perhaps because immense liability issues hinge on recognizing environmental illnesses, and because recognition would implicate most of our institutions and businesses, medicine and government are proceeding cautiously, if not downright reluctantly. Critics complain they are holding chemical-related illnesses to a higher standard of proof than for other health problems.

The fact that most MCS sufferers are women certainly doesn't help. Historically, less attention has been paid to women's health problems than men's, with few studies conducted on them. And physicians diagnose women patients with hysteria two to seven times more often than men. At one extreme end of the spectrum of physicians are doctors who believe MCS is an anxiety disorder or a form of phobia about chemicals. One physician has written that 80 percent of MCS sufferers are women and that MCS-like symptoms were "first described by Hippocrates about three hundred years B.C. …and he called it hysteria and attributed it to the peculiar nature of women."

Other physicians, however, appear to think there is something to MCS but they don't want to go on record about it. At the other end of the spectrum are physicians like Dr. Cunningham who believe toxic overload is one of the most common reasons for diminished health.

Before my illness, I believed the 21st century was too enlightened for us to ignore valid emerging health problems. But MCS taught me that this very human tendency to ignore persists. Much of today's battle over recognizing environmental illnesses seems more political than scientific. When it comes to chemicals' effect on human health, in some ways we still think the earth is flat.

East Meets West

Soon after I started seeing Dr. Cunningham, my life began to improve. Not only did the doctor suggest therapies, diet changes and vitamins to stimulate healing, but he could advise me on practical matters like the best laundry soap to buy or where to get the best air filters. Even when he didn't have a ready answer for my questions, Dr. Cunningham's guesses were worthwhile, owing to his experience with more than a thousand chemically ill patients.

Since Dr. Cunningham's nurses had once been much sicker from MCS themselves, they could also offer me useful suggestions. Through dealing with them, I saw that the quality of medical care could be improved by hiring nurses who had the same health problems as their patients. Dr. Cunningham's nurses had an extra dimension of commitment and practical knowledge that came from having MCS themselves; and they never forgot to call me back or dismissed my concerns. Just meeting them and knowing they now led fairly normal lives reassured me.

Indeed, my most pressing want – short of a cure or control of my symptoms – was help with sorting through the endless daily problems, and with learning how to make the best of the situation. The relentless mysterious reactions were wearing me down. What caused this latest flare-up? Was the latest therapy making me more sensitive to food? It was like having a big tangled pile of string in front of me. I had to laboriously sort through it, day after day, and try to unravel the mess. It was clear I desperately needed help. Even if Dr. Cunningham couldn't control my disease, his suggestions for managing and influencing it improved the quality of my life.

I could see how some doctors might not be cut out for this type of medicine. They would want more clear-cut answers from lab tests and to see quicker results. Dr. Cunningham's method took infinite patience, which he possessed in abundance, and the willingness to keep trying one thing after another. Most of us want easy, painless answers and quick fixes. We tend to get frustrated by drawn-out problems with long-term solutions.

When I first met Dr. Cunningham, I didn't know what to expect. After all, he was the doctor that IME Dr. Lonsdorf had referred to as a charlatan. A softspoken man with sandy-colored hair, Dr. Cunningham had initially started out in family practice in Alaska. But he had quickly grown discouraged. "While I was addressing symptoms," he told me, "I wasn't really getting to understand the patients' root problems. I thought there had to be some better way, so I started reading nutritional books, everything I could find written by MDs and PhDs." As we sat in his office, an air filter hummed in the corner on the cork floor. Behind him, a large window overlooked a grove of poplar trees. This was the only office I could go into without feeling sick. "Then I decided I wanted to learn about nutrition, but I couldn't find any place in the country to study it. That's when I heard of a Dr. Theron Randolph, a Harvard-trained allergist who practiced in Chicago."

Very sick people from all over the country with bad allergies, severe arthritis, asthma and depression sought Dr. Randolph's help. Dr. Cunningham ended up spending one-and-a-half years with him. In Randolph's hospital unit, patients were placed in environmentally controlled rooms, constructed with steel, tile and glass, and sealed by double doors. After five days of fasting on water, 90 percent of them experienced improvement. And of those whose conditions were unchanged, 5 percent grew better after another five days in this unit. Dr. Cunningham grew especially intrigued when these patients were re-introduced to food and chemicals.

Most patients, he told me, had reactions to some common food they ate every day. These physical responses were followed through observation and patients' blood work and pulse measurements. "Some people," Dr. Cunningham recalled, "didn't have reactions until the third or fourth time a food was introduced. Then you'd see changes in their emotions — irritability, depression. Towards the end, we would test them with chemicals in a booth, and I couldn't believe how many people reacted to pesticides, to gas from kitchen stoves, to formaldehyde."

Having a lot of respect for Dr. Randolph's work, but wondering how scientific it was, Dr. Cunningham then studied occupational medicine at a university for two years. "From my studies, I learned that environmental pathology and toxicology fit with Dr. Randolph's program. This was a form of medicine where, instead of handing out aspirin for a headache, you found out what caused it. That's what excited me." He paused and smiled. "Until then, I had been discouraged about medicine, but now I was reborn. And I loved it. It's a difficult and challenging form of healthcare, but it's more patient-oriented. Just a better method for me."

After reviewing my voluminous medical chart and ordering a few additional tests, Dr. Cunningham explained, "Anne, I think you have multiple chemical sensitivity and chronic fatigue syndrome. Basically, I see you as a healthy person who got into trouble by breathing lousy air. We breathe a huge amount of air each day — about 2,000 liters. The lower the quality of air, the harder it is on your system. The poor air in the District building appears to have overtaxed your system. Usually your adrenal glands and your detoxification system can clear out enough chemicals at the end of a day, but poor air can damage those systems. Then toxins pile up and you can't get rid of them anymore."

"When you see people getting sick from their workplaces, what do you typically see?" I asked.

"Respiratory problems, sinus irritation, stuffy noses, headaches, bronchitis, sore throats, post-nasal drip, eye irritation. Those are fairly typical. Then I get a lot of people with cognitive problems: They can't think well, their memory is impaired, they're depressed, irritable, or foggy-headed. I see a lot of that. Or some people will say, 'I get a cold every three weeks', and not realize it is caused by their building. Some event usually triggers a condition like yours — like moving to a bad building or a pregnancy or an injury."

"The District staff that aren't having symptoms – how can you tell they're not affected by the air?" I asked.

"You can't. A person might have headaches, but he takes aspirin and gets rid of them. Then later in life he comes down with colitis, and he takes antacids for that. Then after awhile he gets bladder infections, and he takes antibiotics. It is the same problem, changing form, and it will go on and on until he deals with it."

I glanced toward the trees outside the window, trying to remember where I'd heard this before. All at once the thought of acupuncturist Joe Metcalf came to me. He had said the same thing and had talked about how Chinese medicine can draw correlations between seemingly unrelated health symptoms.

Some of Dr. Cunningham's treatments were intended to relieve physical stress on my body, because recovery can be impaired when the healing system is preoccupied with other tasks, like having to process extra chemicals. Simultaneously, his other treatments sought to strengthen me. I began to take what seemed like a truckload of vitamins each day. Eventually the monthly colds and flu that had plagued me since I became ill began to disappear. Because I was allergic to dust, Dr. Cunningham advised keeping a cleaner house to help my immune system settle down. When I did that, my head felt clearer, as if a fog had lifted.

He also suggested a rotation diet because, since becoming chemically ill, my body reacted to more than half of the foods I had once eaten. At my worst, I had lost 22 pounds. Years later, during an unusually severe exacerbation of my digestive problems, I would come close to dying when the flare-up threw my body into a starvation state and my organ systems began shutting down. Essentially the rotation diet involved cutting out the foods I was sensitive to, and not eating any one thing more than once every five days. Since it takes up to four days for a food to clear the intestinal tract, this allows the body to fully recover before that food is ingested again. Months after I started the diet, my symptoms had noticeably lessened.

The bi-monthly "enzyme-potentiated desensitization shots" Dr. Cunningham gave me for a year helped me tolerate foods better. Each shot, Dr. Cunningham explained, contained minute amounts of 75 major allergens. They were such tiny doses that they were closer to a homeopathic formula than an allergy shot; these injections seemed to stimulate production of T-suppressor cells which subdued the immune system. I loathed the lifestyle changes I had to make for three weeks around each shot to help make it effective. Remembering all the dos and don'ts crammed into the 30-page instruction booklet proved impossible. I just did my best.

Writing the instructions down in my appointment calendar helped. Once, my system went awry when I left my appointment calendar at the acupuncturist's office. The receptionist there read me the next few days of my appointments over the telephone, her voice cool and professional: "Get out special sea salt on Saturday, no sex beginning Sunday, no feather pillow. ..." Suddenly I remembered that it was the week before an EPD shot. I hung up the phone laughing. Ted, who had overheard this, was shaking his head in amusement.

Several years would pass before I heard that Dr. Cunningham had been harassed by the Department of Labor & Industries, which ran the workers' compensation program. When I asked Dr. Cunningham about it, his jaw tightened. "Yes, it's true," he said, looking past me, as if he found the memory unpleasant. "They registered complaints against me to the Medical Disciplinary Board. L&I said I had done this treatment and that test and that they weren't proper medical care so I needed to be investigated. The surprising thing was that they used examples of some of my patients who had been happy with my care – unbeknownst to them." Dr. Cunningham sat forward in his chair. "They did this to me five times. I dealt with one complaint, then a second, but they just kept coming. The complaints not only cost me a lot of money in legal fees, but I had to spend my weekends writing the equivalent of a master's thesis to defend myself."

Dr. Cunningham argued that the complaints were a scientific debate that didn't belong in disciplinary hearings. He charged that he wasn't doing anything illegal. In fact, he said, he was treating a segment of the population that others didn't want to deal with. He considered the complaints harassment and countered that he was considering a lawsuit against the Medical Disciplinary Board and L&I.

"L&I stopped," he said. "I haven't heard from them for about a year now."

❧

For a brief time, I also consulted a Western physician who incorporated Ayurveda medicine into his practice. This doctor saw me as very sick, and while he could help me, he cautioned that I would need to do more than Ayurvedic suggestions to recover. One of the oldest medical systems in the world, Ayurveda is still used today in India, alongside Western medicine; it combines meditation, diet, herbs, minerals and aromas to create balance, which, in turn, stimulates health. Particular emphasis is placed upon enhancing digestion. Although I primarily used the acupuncturist's and environmental medicine doctor's recommendations to heal, many Ayurvedic guidelines made me feel so much better that to this day they remain part my routine.

The recommendations included eating warm meals, emphasizing easily digestible foods that were best for my individual constitution; eating my main meal of the day at noon; lights out by 10 p.m., because this time of day is most conducive to restful sleep and to effective digestion; and walks outside each day. Some Ayurvedic suggestions overlapped with acupuncture's. Of course, I couldn't possibly follow every healthcare provider's advice completely. Sometimes their recommendations even contradicted each other. The Ayurvedic diet, for instance, suggested eating rice or wheat daily, but through Dr. Cunningham I had discovered that my body reacted to wheat. I merely did what I could, incorporating the ideas that seemed to work best.

Meditation ended up being a useful part of the Ayurvedic program. Although I had practiced insight meditation on and off for years, it now had become a daily practice. Many think meditating means getting rid of unwanted thoughts and feelings, or that it will lead to feeling good all the time. Instead, meditation is about the mind staying open, relaxed, and in the present. It is a form of undistracted awareness that helps us live each moment as fully as we can, to see things as they really are. In the end, practicing meditation and paying attention to how I lived and ate seemed to coax my body toward health.

112

Eating, sleeping and meditating at roughly the same time every day took some discipline, but the rhythm it created produced a sense of harmony in the way that Eastern medicine used nature's rhythms, the ebb and flow of seasons, and alternation between day and night for its foundation to produce a calming, healing influence. This is the sort of experience that is difficult to achieve with the erratic schedules that often accompany urban life. The rhythm merely reinforced my growing connection to nature.

Following all these health recommendations took an enormous amount of time. Just preparing cooked meals from scratch, eating them slowly, and cleaning up the kitchen consumed a significant chunk of the day. But I digested food better as a result, and I didn't feel so exhausted. My diet required frequent trips to the grocery and health food stores. No single place carried all the ingredients and vitamins I needed, and because the few things I could eat were not common foods, stores were often out of stock. Running around from one store to another tired me. Locating four different protein powders that I could tolerate – since taking the same one every day caused reactions – was an exasperating process. For the protein powders alone, I had to go to three different stores. Getting plenty of sleep and taking naps also took extra hours each day. Often I could savor the kindergarten post-lunch-nap feel of my one-to-two-hour siestas; but sometimes they seemed like sinkholes in my day. Some days I'd sleep, eat, attend a healthcare appointment – and that would be the day.

Ted and some of our friends wondered whether I should try so many things. From their perspectives, I could see why they felt that way. Some days I asked the same question myself. But from my viewpoint, no single health system or provider had all the answers – that had become crystal clear. Exploring uncharted territory was a confusing business; and stumbling from one provider to the next, finding that each could offer me only limited help, was one of the loneliest feelings I'd ever known. Many of the therapies offered some relief in a way the others did not. Besides, if I were to try only one therapy at a time, I might discover that the only remedy I'd done all year hadn't worked, or that it alone hadn't done enough to bring about a significant improvement. The process could take much longer and my health might slip even further in the meantime.

It would have been helpful to have hindsight about which therapies would be most effective. But no one could offer me that. Doing nothing but avoiding chemicals and getting rest alone hadn't gotten me anywhere. So into the murky darkness I plunged. Then I pieced together a patchwork quilt of trial-and-error remedies, hoping the overall pattern would look like healing in the end.

My food sensitivities had made meals seem more like medicine than pleasure. Ted and I had always split up making meals, but the duty now became my province. Figuring out which ingredients I could eat on a particular day was complicated for another person to do. Besides, I was the one at home all day. When my weight kept dropping month after month, I knew that meals had to entice me more. Second helpings of plain millet or quinoa, where was the pleasure in that? Cooking meals then grew into a stimulating creative challenge – not only for my own survival but to free me from having to make separate dishes for Ted. I learned how to use a pressure cooker. Stacks of cookbooks from the library began to grace our living room; many cuisines from the Caribbean to Asia offered wheat-and-dairy-free recipes that could be adapted to my diet. One winter night, with dinner only an hour away, I stared at a jar of white beans wondering how I could possibly dress them up so Ted wouldn't wrinkle his nose at them. Out came the white porcelain soufflé dishes. Fresh rosemary from the garden, a splash of white wine, and a few diced tomatoes later, I sprinkled the flavored beans with sautéed breadcrumbs. When Ted asked, "What's for dinner?" I gave it a French-sounding name – white bean gratin. It sounded more elegant than plain old baked beans. "Wow," he said, perking up. Sometimes it was the details that mattered.

૨૭

Nearly three years after starting the therapies, I was strong enough to try detoxification – getting chemicals out of my body. Dr. Cunningham had long ago suggested gentler cleansing methods, but each attempt had only left me sicker. For instance, weeks after starting L-reduced glutathione, an amino acid that stimulates the liver to expel toxins, I was throwing up all my food and water, although my colon certainly felt cleaned out. It was like riding on a runaway train. Even cutting back to one-fifth of the capsule had the same effect. So I gave up on cleansing for the time being.

At first, the concept of detoxifying had seemed far-fetched. But I became convinced there was something to it because after trying one cleansing method after another, I would get the exact same symptoms. Homeopathic detoxification powders, glutathione, Ayurvedic methods – all produced a surface headache on the top of my head like a brick weighing me down, nausea and vomiting, and lightheadedness that made the room appear to vibrate.

The sign on the door to the detoxification clinic read, *Our chemically sensitive patients cannot tolerate scented toiletries or cosmetics, perfumes, colognes, aftershave, etc. Please do not wear these products into this office! Thanks!* I had chosen this provider because of his careful, comprehensive approach. After so many unsuccessful attempts, I was desperate for the cleansing to work.

This was no ordinary office. Inside, doors looked out onto an open area with a sauna. In the corner above a purified water cooler, shelves were packed with vitamins, electrolyte tablets and food powders. The bathrooms included showers and lockers. Dr. John Burgess, a naturopath with brown hair and a graying beard, led me into his office crammed with books. I sat in the green leather chair opposite his desk feeling tempered hope, but also annoyed at having to tell my story to yet another person, to try one more therapy, to spend more money. Dr. Burgess explained that the liver is the organ most directly strained by pollution and environmental damage. He told me that with an illness like mine, a vital liver is key. Among the functions this organ performs is removing chemicals from circulation and then detoxifying them. While experts knew that alcohol could damage the liver, they didn't understand much about what chemicals did to it. A thorough detoxification of the body, he continued, had helped MCS patients like me as well as people with diseases like lupus, Parkinson's disease, chronic Epstein-Barr virus, and conditions induced by silicone breast implants. When blood tests were done on healthy people exposed to solvents, Dr. Burgess explained, the chemicals usually cleared out of the patients' bodies within hours. At most it might take a couple of days. But in patients with conditions like MCS or cancer, tests indicated that their bodies didn't get rid of them nearly as fast, and sometimes not at all. It's as if those people have a defect in their system, but it's not clear where.

Dr. Burgess didn't suggest his usual program for me, though. My body was too fragile. Typically patients spent five days a week at his clinic for a month. The program included moderate exercise, three hours a day in a low-heat sauna, hydrotherapy, colon cleansings, and short breaks for rest and electrolyte replacement. He did propose the same series of pre-detoxification therapies other patients got, to make certain that my body had the tools it needed to cleanse itself: A treatment using acupressure would help me absorb certain vitamins and essential oils; psyllium husk powder would bind the toxins in my bowel and make elimination more efficient; and hydrotherapy – hot and cold towels alternated on my chest – would boost my immune system. Then Dr. Burgess prescribed weekly colonics to gently clean out my colon with water. In a year, he said, the level of chemicals in my blood tests would tell him whether I needed to continue the colonics, and if so, for how long.

Never before had I seen such immediate progress. Once I began the colonics, the pace of healing went from a creep to a crawl. Within a month, I was eating 30 percent more food, needing an hour less sleep each night, and eliminating my two-hour post-lunch naps. My arthritis had improved, especially in my chest. I actually had two hours of energy most mornings. Until then I couldn't even remember what having energy felt like. The downside was that it took me three days to recover from each colonic. It was like having the flu for half the week on top of my usual health problems, only to have to return and start the process all over again. Nevertheless, shortly after beginning detoxification, I walked around feeling as if I was in a dream. At first I restrained myself from getting too excited. Maybe it wouldn't last. After all, some people had not found it helpful. But eventually I couldn't ignore what was happening. Then I started to feel giddy.

I'd like to say the colonics brought steady uphill progress. But after five, flare-ups began occurring. When they happened, they were big: blinding headaches, vomiting, a heightened sensitivity to chemicals and food, weakness, and severe constipation. My weight dropped 10 pounds. I didn't know it at the time, but it would take two years for my digestive system to recover. Trying colonics would be the biggest mistake I made. In the meantime, I felt crestfallen. Aggressive therapies clearly were not for me. As he helped clean up the aftermath, acupuncturist Joe Metcalf observed, "Your body doesn't like to be pushed in a direction. Even in acupuncture, I cannot make your body do anything. All I can do is give you the tools and let it do the work." Thus, in the end acupuncture and vitamins became my long-term therapies. Once again, I reluctantly accepted that the road to recovery would be slowly paved.

The colonics brought about changes in how I approached future health treatments. From then on, I ran every therapy that I was considering past Dr. Cunningham. Maybe hard medical studies didn't exist, but at least Dr. Cunningham had heard of most remedies for MCS and he could share what he'd learned about them. If I had only asked him in the first place, Dr. Cunningham would have explained that some of his patients had gotten worse after trying colonics. As a result, he didn't recommend them. Thus, I added a set of criteria to consider before trying anything new. Any treatment that involved getting sicker before getting better, I would no longer do. Even mainstream medicine takes that approach sometimes – like giving chemotherapy to cancer patients – but my fragile system couldn't afford the getting-worse part. Also, it now helped to see new healthcare providers, even mainstream doctors, as potential risks to my health. New practitioners couldn't simply read my chart or listen to my history to get a good grasp of my condition. They had to put in time with me in the trenches before they weren't potentially dangerous.

The lack of good medical studies in alternative care continued to frustrate me. I can safely say that meandering through this "alternative" world was like being in the Wild West where anything goes. I began to appreciate the rigorous system medicine had to evaluate treatments and theories. Many alternative healthcare providers, I discovered, had no idea when they were hurting people – because when a practitioner's remedy harmed a person, the patient often didn't go back to tell him. When I told Dr. Burgess about how sick I was because of his treatments, he seemed genuinely shocked and claimed that this had never happened before. Yet Dr. Cunningham had had a number of patients whose health was damaged by detoxification treatments at Dr. Burgess' clinic.

Setbacks like the colonics episode always made me rethink my course. Was it worth my while to forage through this wild continent of alternative healthcare? A strength of the mainstream medical community, I would muse, was that physicians weren't afraid to debate openly among themselves, or to stand firm until they understood a health problem within their paradigm before treating patients. What would you rather have, I would ask myself, because the downside of the scientific approach was that it was slow to recognize new health problems and not everything could be proved scientifically. In this country we often cling to the myth that knowledge proved by science is the only truth worth knowing. If it weren't for alternative healthcare, I'd think, I might be dead or an invalid. I would usually end up appreciating that I had both systems to choose from, imperfect as they were.

How I often wished that healthcare providers from all disciplines could at least converge and share their knowledge about chemically ill patients. Going from one health system to another, I saw that people in each field had expertise to contribute to the dialogue. Our understanding of chemical illnesses would improve if this knowledge could be brought together.

Next, two events occurred which showed me the limitations of relying too heavily on medical tests. A doctor sent me to endocrinologist Dr. Betts because so many of my symptoms were consistent with thyroid trouble. Time after time, doctors had tested my thyroid, but the results always came back within the very large statistical normal range. Not everyone, Dr. Betts explained, showed up on standard thyroid tests. He was going to have to use a different one for me. The test used in the past defined a statistically normal range, but some people with abnormal thyroids fell outside that normal range. Not all endocrinologists, he said, agreed on this issue. I think you've got an under-active thyroid, called hypothyroidism, Dr. Betts said while feeling my neck. You've got many of the common symptoms like yellowish skin, fatigue, muscle aches, and feeling cold.

Sure enough, the test results indicated an under-active thyroid. When I first took the prescribed medication, it felt as if someone had turned on a light bulb in the dark recesses of my interior. Within weeks, my digestion improved, my muscles ached less, and seemingly unrelated problems like bumps on my eyelids went away. With time, other symptoms declined as well.

Trying to chart my health problems with tests was like trying to map the Bermuda triangle, I complained to Ted. Wasn't it ironic, I waxed on, that the IME doctors who were working overtime trying to come up with reasons for my health troubles that didn't involve the District building couldn't diagnose a common thyroid condition? How dare they tell me that my problems were in my head when they hadn't ruled everything out? Ted would listen patiently, though with some weariness. There was nothing else to say.

And there were more underlying health problems that had gone undiagnosed. Muscle spasms broke out throughout my body, causing intensive-care-level pain. Just getting my legs over the side of the bed in the morning caused me to burst into tears. Since getting MCS, I had suffered from muscle spasms that were like weeklong charley horses, but this was different. You may have an electrolyte imbalance, my physical therapist had told me. So off I shuffled to the doctor, dragging my leg behind me like a well-worn stuffed animal with all the fuzziness worn off. But the electrolyte test came back normal.

Still, the problem continued unabated. I had to take a hot bath every hour, even throughout the night, just to manage the pain. In a fit of exasperation, I bought some electrolyte drink. If medicine didn't always have a sensitive enough barometer to test my body, then trial and error seemed the next best thing, as long as it couldn't hurt me. Within an hour of the first electrolyte drink, my muscle spasms began subsiding. While I was relieved, the experience also made me wonder what other common medical problems I might have that were going undetected.

A Small Body of Hope

In my next therapy session with Sally Newell, I brought up the subject of hope. "These days I'm struggling with how to have hope in a constructive way. When the colonics were helping the first five weeks, I was so sure they were going to bump the quality of my life upward. But some forms of hope, even optimism, seem to be a denial of reality. Are hope and optimism sometimes a cover for not being able to accept your life the way it really is?"

Sally looked into the distance and thought for a minute. The pale afternoon rays of the sun threw a golden light across her face like a spotlight illuminating a sculpture. Sally reached for her dictionary.

"Hope," she read, "is the expectation of something desired." She looked up. "If your doctor gives you hope in the right way, he reaches for the Biblical kind. He might say, 'This condition is bad but don't give up hope. Try to eat well and get plenty of rest. Keep up your emotional health if you can. But the outcome for your disease is unpredictable.' The kind of hope you've been pursuing puts you in a bind of being unrealistic. I want to teach you how to hope when you've got a dark picture."

I reached for my notebook. With my memory problems, writing thoughts down helped me retain what we talked about.

"Human beings need to have something to do with their minds — some way to put their minds at rest — when the future is uncertain." Sally paused thoughtfully. "You need to discipline yourself. When you notice improvement in your health, feel good about it briefly. But instead of thinking that you'll be able to eat chocolate in a few months or work in a year, maintain a sense of doubt and uncertainty. Say to yourself that you don't know what you'll be doing in a year. Then wish that you can work part-time in a year and wonder if you'll be able to do it."

"It doesn't help me that our culture constantly sends out messages that I can will my way to health if only I can get control of my thoughts and emotions," I said.

"There are people who say they want to make a million dollars by the time they're 40, and some actually do," Sally observed. "But if they believe that only their minds brought it about, they are fools. A lot of other things went into helping them make their first million."

❧

Pursuing alternative therapies consumed not just time, but also an enormous amount of money. None of them was covered by health insurance. Being chemically ill was expensive. Each year, Ted and I had $11,000 in additional bills, although the first year it was $18,000 – for healthcare, air and water filters, special products, and organic food – at a time when I wasn't working. If I could get out of the vitamin store without spending several hundred dollars, I was relieved. I would joke to Ted that I could write a book about how to live like a monk on the expenses of a millionaire. Fortunately I had the disability insurance payments during part of this time, because of my exacerbated arthritis. And we had rent from our boarder.

"Do you think any of this is helping?" Ted would frequently ask, exasperated, as if he suspected I was wasting our money. Progress was too slow, the effects too subtle, the path too uncharted, for him to notice. One night I answered the question by giving him an example of how the therapies were working. I felt like I'd woken up from a nap within hours of starting my vitamin B complex, I said. But Ted didn't altogether believe me. All he had for proof was my words.

"I want to see a full accounting of what all this is costing us," he said, sitting up straighter on the sofa, clenching his fists. "Where is all the money going?" I went to fetch my checkbook.

"Acupuncture," I read, "food, gas, vitamins. ..." The conversation ended with no resolution. Sometimes moments like this made me wonder if I would be better off on my own. I loved Ted dearly, more than words could say. My feelings for him only grew stronger with each passing year. But knowing how my health affected Ted's life daily, and having to make an effort to be sociable around him when I felt rotten, took a toll. In other moments, though, I felt that Ted's and my relationship brought me so much joy that it made all the difference during these trying times. But sometimes I still wondered if it would be easier for us to be apart; and I worried at how my illness was increasingly becoming more difficult for us as a couple.

Healthcare bills didn't diminish over time. Years into MCS, I began to think that while my therapies had brought improvements, they didn't seem like they would be enough to help me reach maximum healing. That's when I learned about Pam Brigg. Pam was an acupuncturist who used a new method she had devised that she called allergy relief systems, which used acupressure to treat allergies and sensitivities. It was an approach that had similarities with a treatment called NAET (Nambudripad's Allergy Elimination Techniques).

The first time I saw Pam, my stomach problems were so aggravated that I drove to her office with a bowl and towel in my lap, hoping to make it there without throwing up. Since contracting MCS, my health had declined dramatically toward the end of August each year. It was as if someone threw a grenade down my stomach and it wreaked havoc until sometime in the spring. Windy days were worse, so I guessed that some allergen was involved. On the roughest days, I hunkered down indoors with air filters going at full blast. The house would sound like an airplane getting ready for takeoff.

Pam greeted me at the door and ushered me into the chair next to her desk. After listening to my history, she said, "I'm going to see if I can figure out what your body is reacting to most today. But I've got to warn you that my treatment may not be as effective because you are in the middle of such a strong reaction." My heart sank at the news. Pam motioned me over to the examining table and asked me to lie on my back. Next she handed me a series of glass vials as she held my wrist. "I'm feeling your pulse, Anne," she said, "to measure your *chi* or life force energy. If your *chi* shows imbalance when you're holding one of these substances, it means you're reacting to it." I didn't talk or ask questions because the mere effort increased the fire of my nausea.

"What's coming up today are molds and funguses," Pam said. All at once I remembered I had been allergic to mold as a little girl. "You react so strongly to them that I can only clear one variety of fungus today." Pam handed me a vial with the offending substance in it. She pressed several points on my head, then felt my pulse again to see what her treatment had accomplished. "OK, your body is now in balance in relationship to this fungus. Let's hope you feel better."

Part of me wanted to laugh. That's it? I wanted to say. You touch my head and the treatment is over? I drove home hoping the session would help me but fearing it might be a blind alley.

Within hours, however, my nausea was subsiding. No other treatment had pulled me out of a severe place so quickly. I felt elated. Following through with Pam's full program, though, was like embarking on an archaeological dig because she had to clear me for so many things. Earthquake reactions kept occurring followed by aftershocks. Pam would patiently have to figure out what had caused them. She had to clear some substances that I reacted severely to, like mold, several times. The whole process would take more than a year of weekly appointments. Pam believed her work might take several years to take full effect. In the meantime, my seasonal allergies had calmed down enough that my general illness symptoms seemed more like background music than loud rock and roll blaring in my ears.

With the quality of my daily life still dim, I decided to learn Chi Gong – an ancient Chinese practice, similar to yoga, using body movement to promote health and healing – to help me manage day-to-day life better. Chi Gong worked with *chi*, the same life force energy as in acupuncture and Pam's treatments. Eventually, once I'd learned Chi Gong and related Eastern-healing methods well enough through Jennifer Browne, I went to acupuncture less often. I got similar results on my own, and on a daily basis.

Jennifer had first been intrigued with Eastern healing practices when she was just 17 years old. She left the East Coast for California in the late 1960s to learn more about those health systems. Later she taught classes in Eastern healing herself. But the best way, others advised Jennifer, to learn about Eastern healing methods was from strict traditional Tao masters, rather than from Westerners. Tao was an ancient Chinese philosophy of life that derived its learning from nature. The old Tao masters also functioned as healing agents, practicing healing arts like acupuncture and Chi Gong. A Tao master, who had moved from China to North Hollywood in the late 1950s, took Jennifer on as an apprentice for two years.

After that Jennifer heard about another Tao Master from Taiwan, who was also living in California. The Tao Master told Jennifer that if 10 people were interested, he would teach a two-year course in Tao meditation practices from which Chi Gong, acupuncture, and other healing methods sprung. This was no ordinary course. Each day Jennifer would follow a highly disciplined program, rising at 3 a.m. to sit meditating for two hours. At 5 a.m. she and other students did a two-hour meditation while walking; from 7 a.m. to 9 a.m. Jennifer sat in a tree meditating; at sunset she did Chi Gong or Tai Chi. By 7:30 p.m. she was ready for bed. By the end of the two years, Jennifer and the other students wanted to learn more, so they continued the course for another three years.

During my first appointment with Jennifer, she explained the approach she would use with me. She told me she wanted to teach me how to generate my own life-force energy and to get it circulating. She noted that *chi* in people with chronic diseases doesn't circulate throughout their bodies well. So one must learn to do manually what healthy bodies do automatically. Exercise helps generate and circulate *chi*, so she recommended I do it five times a week. I listened intently and shifted in my chair. This was similar to acupuncture but somehow different.

Jennifer stressed finding my own deep strength through my body's inherent center. She said this would help me become more grounded and centered and that it would spill over into the rest of my life – help give me more control of my life.

Jennifer put it this way: "If I could take an energetic snapshot of most people, you'd see scattered pieces of energy all over the place. Have you heard of the expressions being 'grounded' and 'centered'?" I nodded. "When that happens, a snapshot would show those scattered pieces of energy becoming consolidated, then anchored to the earth. All of a person's bodily systems run more healthfully from that grounded place."

She told me to stand up. "Start with your arms down in front of you, with your hands slightly cupped." She demonstrated the position. "Now slowly raise them up to your breast bone, keeping your hands about an inch from your body." I brought my hands up. "No, you're going too fast. You can't hold the energy that you're generating as well that way." I started again, this time in slow motion. Next she told me that once I got to my breast area, to extend my hands outward, then bring them back to my breast and down to the starting point. Very slowly. When my hands passed over my stomach, I heard gurgling, much like the sound I heard in acupuncture. Inside me it felt like tiny champagne bubbles were rising to the surface. "You're doing it," Jennifer said, smiling. "Well done. Can you feel the *chi* being generated?" I nodded. "Now walk around the room to circulate the energy."

On the way home that day, I felt as if I'd been on a brisk walk – not tired, but as if everything in me flowed like a smooth, deep river. After months of practicing Chi Gong daily, I noticed that afterward I had more energy and tolerated chemicals better. So I began to deliberately time my Chi Gong practice to occur just before going someplace that would aggravate my health, like to my book group. Doing this practice felt like I was giving myself gentle acupuncture every day. To make room for it, I cut back on meditation as well as acupuncture because Chi Gong and other Eastern healing methods Jennifer taught me were accomplishing roughly the same thing. To make the practices effective, you had to focus only on the moment, just as in meditation.

But soon I discovered that even Jennifer's methods could make me worse if I wasn't careful. If the work was too strong, it generated more energy than my body could handle, just as in acupuncture when Joe used too many needles. Jennifer adjusted her recommendations and the problem went away. She had to be more cautious with me just as my doctors and other healthcare providers did.

Despite my frustrations with the limitations and therapies, my body began to improve slowly and steadily. Plenty of rest provided the glue that held my healing together. I napped throughout each day and slept as long as I wanted to at night, about 10 to 11 hours. Rest alone hadn't been enough to bring about improvement, but without it my therapies didn't work nearly as well. As I began to feel better, my anger toward the workers' compensation process faded; and other people's skepticism about my alternative therapies bothered me less. Regaining my health mattered more than anything else.

I added small amounts of foods back like oatmeal, tomatoes and wheat – although, like other foods, none of them could be eaten more than once every five days. I noticed promising benchmarks: One day following a haircut in a salon, I actually slept through the night. Eventually my body only needed two days to recover from a dentist appointment, instead of the usual week.

Even my mental problems had improved a little. I realized this one night while talking to neighbors at our annual block barbecue. People up and down the street had streamed into my front garden carrying hot dogs, watermelons, and bowls of potato salad. Several men hoisted their picnic tables and benches over the hedge. Others rolled grills into the street behind a sawhorse that said the block would be closed to traffic until 10 p.m. Several children, their mouths stained with blackberry juice, called out, "Anne, watch us roll down the hill!" I stopped a moment to watch them wriggling down a sloped part of the lawn. Mercifully, the sun had begun to set, leaving the yard in the cool shadow of a towering evergreen tree.

While talking to several neighbors about their summer fishing trips, I was surprised to hear myself use words like "prowess" and "disclaimer." These were the kind of precise words that had eluded me for years. Usually I felt tongue-tied, frustrated, wanting to use a certain word but unable retrieve it. I was relieved to know that even this could change.

ూ

Finally Ted and I could plan a vacation to my friend Cindy Levy's old farmhouse in Ashland, Oregon, where we would be alone for the first few days before Cindy joined us. Thanks to MCS, traveling with me had become as complicated as with an infant so we practically needed a trailer to cart along all that I would need. Packing my breakfast food and vitamins took two hours alone. Since away from home I grew sicker, as I was exposed to a higher pollution level than in my home and the car exhaust from a long drive sickened me, the challenge was to keep the exacerbation manageable, so that I could feel well enough to have fun. Once we reached Ashland's valley, its rounded hills covered with velvet green down and windswept trees, Ted and I felt uplifted by the bucolic setting. We sat in Cindy's glass-enclosed living room, drinking in the rippling valley and Lake Immigrant stretched below us. Geese waddled about Cindy's pond, horses dozed in the meadow, and sheep grazed peacefully on distant hills. We telephoned Cindy. I said, "You're going to have trouble getting us out of here!"

Despite my pleasure at being there, a burning headache and stinging chest pain plagued me. Every breath provoked stabs of searing pain. Lying down at night magnified my chest pain so much that I could barely turn over. I lay still for hours, grieving over the fact that taking a vacation always worsened my health. Not long ago, life had not been like this. Vacations had been among the highlights of my year. Still, it had been worth it to come, if only because Ted and I needed a change of scene together. I lay there straddled between knowing it was a good thing to come and wishing that I were at home. Eventually my eye lids grew leaden and my thoughts gave way to slumber.

Each month during this time, I telephoned my director, Nancy Murdoch, as she had asked me to do. I always dreaded making those calls. It felt like reporting in from war trenches to someone who had a desk job back in Iowa. Knowing that my illness had repercussions for others troubled me, and I didn't like being reminded there was still a world going on, a world I had once been a part of. I had told Nancy several times how much I appreciated her suggestion to take a year's leave of absence; she would thank me for being open to the plan.

I always put down the telephone feeling unsettled. Hopefully, I would think, I'll return to work soon.

The Biggest Challenge of All

It turned out that the bureaucrats and medical examiners weren't the only people who didn't want to hear about my illness. Friends, acquaintances and co-workers – some of them had trouble accepting a health problem that couldn't be easily proved or cured. A murky illness, I was learning, draws skepticism out of people like water from a new well. Doubt only rose when my health troubles continued long after I had left my office. And coping with these skeptical reactions created a second layer of suffering that proved to be a tougher, less straightforward, challenge than the disease itself.

Some people would simply grow bored and impatient with a condition that stretched on year after year. Others cast blame or judgment, often through subtle forms of unasked-for advice. My lifestyle and personality were relentlessly analyzed, interpreted and found to be wanting. My illness was often seen as a personal failing. I must have done something wrong to allow this illness to take hold of my life, the talk implied. Perhaps if I could think more positively or relax and handle stress better, I wouldn't have such an array of health problems. Or maybe I worried too much about my body. Comfortably removed from the chaotic, daily reality of MCS, these self-appointed experts were fortunate to not fully understand the kind of physical suffering that brings you to your knees.

Reactions to my illness generally fell into two categories. One group could empathize – or could at least be humble and entertain the possible existence of a health condition that hadn't happened to them. The other group could not. We all can deny what we don't want to believe, but some do it more forcefully than others.

When others questioned my illness, or doubted I was handling the situation well, I wanted to let them know I needed time and space to adapt to the losses in my life. Each limitation imposed by my body felt like a death. Life as I had known it had ended. And additional losses continued to pile up year after year. With an illness this wild, one that affected every facet of my life, it took me years to get my sea legs, so to speak.

What I want people to understand is that chemically ill people aren't alone in finding that their illnesses attract moral judgment and uninvited advice. My story, in many ways, is not so far removed from those of people with other kinds of lengthy illnesses. People suffering with everything from cancer to asthma have written and talked about similar experiences to mine. However, with a sickness like MCS, which hasn't been officially recognized by mainstream medicine and society, the judgments and reactions tend to get even more extreme. Why is lingering illness subject to so much self-righteous condemnation? I've often wondered. Why is it attributed to psychosomatic causes, or why is the victim seen as not having enough willpower? Could it be that defining illness in this way makes curing disease seem easy and straightforward, more under our control, and therefore less threatening? Whatever the reason, I've noticed that the less we understand a health problem, the more we tend to blame its sufferers. Too often, the "positive attitude" advice is just another form of reproach.

Some of the "attitude" talk really made my teeth ache. "Having a good attitude improves your health," people would say from their ivory towers of good health. I'd reply, "Maybe, but once you get sick you'd better have money, and it's amazing what *that* can do for your quality of life and your attitude! Sure, a positive attitude can often help improve the quality of life for people with illnesses but I'm finding it doesn't automatically improve one's health. How I wish it were simply that easy."

I've noticed, after years of living abroad, that we Americans seem to love advice involving simple formulas and one-size-fits-all explanations. We want easy answers and quick results. It's no coincidence that we've brought the world innovations like fast food, shopping malls, and speed dating. One of our most favorite quick and easy remedies for life's problems is the advice that all you have to do is change your thoughts or beliefs and you'll get what you want.

It's not that I don't believe our beliefs and thoughts can help us achieve what we want, because I do. I just don't think beliefs and thoughts alone automatically get you what you want in every situation. If our thoughts and attitudes produced results that simply, there would be many more millionaires or people in perfect health, and everyone who ran for president would get the job. There are many additional factors that go into attaining our dreams.

Many years later, I would find an especially effective Chinese doctor, who practiced Chinese medicine and acupuncture, who used techniques that worked with my thoughts to help foster health – such as visualizing energy blockages being released as I did a breathing meditation. But those techniques were only one of about 15 different therapies she used with me to address my energy blockages and weaknesses. The doctor never implied that changing my thoughts alone would be enough to achieve good health. Chinese medicine has more than 3,000 years of experience with the mind-body connection so I believe its practitioners have a more evolved and nuanced understanding than we do in the United States, where we have only about 30 years of experience with it.

Listening to all the talk and theories, I've often felt like an anthropologist researching health beliefs held by our society. For one thing, Americans have a hard time accepting that life involves pain and suffering. We tend to see health as a right, so when sickness stubbornly eludes a cure, something is wrong with the natural order of things. We come up with theories about why an illness occurs and often decide it's the truth. Ironically, despite our preoccupation in the United States with health and how to attain it, and our insistence that we can find solutions to every problem, we are no healthier than, for instance, the French or the English.

Our health fixation seems part of our culture's love affair with self-improvement. Self-help improvement books comprise more than half of all best-selling nonfiction titles here, yet you can't give them away in most other countries. Believing in progress and assuming we can fix any problem, or have whatever we want, we're perpetually striving to perfect ourselves and improve our lives. On the whole, I think our optimism and can-do spirit is a lovely characteristic of our culture, but when we go overboard to the point that we can't admit some problems may not be solvable – at least not at the present time – we can be an insufferable lot and a suffering lot, for we blame ourselves, too.

Those people skeptical about my illness loved to talk about stress and the mind. *You had a stressful job*, some reminded me, forgetting I had been healthy doing the same work for eight years in the old building. *There is so much we don't know about how the mind affects the body.* Wasn't it more relevant to talk about how little we know about chemicals' effects on human health? When people saw the stress resulting from my illness, they mistook it for the cause. They expected me to adjust to my illness, even have positive feelings about it, as quickly as possible.

Advocates of the "stress automatically causes disease" theory clung to their beliefs with a religious fervor. It has become a favorite catch-all diagnosis for health troubles that can't be readily explained or solved, even among some physicians. There was no reasoning with these folks. One friend, who happened to call me in the middle of a severe gut flare-up, said right away, Have you been upset lately? No, I said. Under a lot of stress? No, I said again. Have you had an upsetting conversation with anyone? She persisted on and on. I marveled at how she missed asking questions about what I might have been exposed to or eaten that could have set off this event. Past experience had taught me not to bring this up since my friend would probably say I was *in denial*. The beauty of the situation was that many of these other people had the luxury of having opinions about my health without being held accountable for them if they were wrong.

My friend's life was no less stressful than mine, yet she was healthy. When people implied that healing just involved handling stress better, it reminded me of when drop-dead gorgeous actresses or supermodels say beauty comes from within, or from finding your inner light. I hate to burst their bubbles, but I could be the happiest, most enlightened person in the world and I still won't be as beautiful as them. Besides, with the right genes, you can be a jerk and still be breathtakingly gorgeous. Likewise, with the right genes you might not handle stress well but you can still be healthy.

Some people, when I vented frustration about the lack of clear answers to my health problems, would cut me off and begin talking brightly about the power of the mind. To avoid unpleasant life experiences, they appeared to anesthetize themselves. Ironically, the most insistent mind-over-matter people struck me as the most afraid of the unknown and of problems that can't be readily solved.

As part of our enthusiasm for health advice, we've created black-and-white categories to define health and sickness. We categorize complex personality characteristics under "Type A" or "Type B," and depending on which article you read, one type is more likely to get sick. Then we tend to notice whatever confirms our bias and disregard what doesn't. Illnesses get discussed as if they are simple recipes. People have heart disease because they don't eat well or exercise enough, or because they bottle up their emotions. If a person is healthy, we see it as proof that she is living right – not that that her body might tolerate more abuse than other people's, or that she's simply lucky. No, we insist, her health demonstrates that she is in control. Who wants to be reminded that life can change you in an instant, for no apparent reason?

This persistent theme of self-control or mind-control, which has seemingly permeated so much of our health talk, partially reflects our Puritanical roots. The Puritans emphasized self-control, especially of the body, with a zealous self-righteousness. Although the Puritans haven't been around for more than a century, today we're still keen on something like this self-mastery, whether it be through efforts to control our minds or the way we try to whip our bodies into athletic shape – or the way we imply that sick people who can't find a cure are practically moral failures.

In recent years, the pendulum has swung hard toward stress and psychological explanations for disease. In part, we're trying to make up for years of being too focused on the body alone. But ironically, while concentrating on the mind, we often split it from the body, perpetuating the same fragmented approach. When trying to correct this body-mind imbalance, we must make sure we don't recreate what we're trying to run away from. Because this is the inescapable paradox: The body and the mind are one; and, at the same time, they are different.

For example, in a recent study, when 47 patients were interviewed about illness and injury, all of them rejected the idea that chance or luck explained why one person got sick and not another. They believed there are good and bad ways of acting, and the bad ones may lead to stress and so to illness. I came to view the mind's influence on illness as one piece in a large puzzle. In certain situations, in some people, that piece was large enough to influence the overall picture of the sickness. But in other cases it was not. As always, from my vantage point, easy single-factor answers remained elusive.

Once ill, I began to see how anxious the thought of losing their health makes people. Strangely enough, at my sickest, I was liberated from that innate fear. I didn't have to worry about it. I was already there. Would this change, I wondered, once my health grew stronger? My situation wasn't like losing a leg or having a loved one die; in those circumstances, at least you have a clear sense of what you must get used to, and your loss is seen and acknowledged by others. But with my illness, the symptoms were always shifting. Living in a state of continuous upheaval had become normal. Whenever I tried the "relax and forget about it" advice, my health took a nose dive. Paying attention was the smartest choice, given my miserable options.

People didn't seem to recognize the implicit blame in their remarks. Sometimes I didn't myself, yet I would wonder why I felt discouraged after talking to them. At other times, the judgments were painfully obvious, like the day I called to ask my friend Melanie if I could use her sewing machine. "Sure, come on over," she had replied. I could hear the din of her children playing in the background. Shortly after beginning to sew in Melanie's basement, though, I felt queasy. Melanie was walking in and out of the room in between loads of laundry. Her daughter appeared to ask if she could eat a Popsicle. I was sewing quickly because the top of my head was growing tighter by the minute, as if someone was pulling me up by my scalp. Something down in the basement was making me sick. Curiously, the upstairs of Melanie's house didn't have the same effect on me. Still, I kept quiet, not wanting to encourage one of Melanie's increasingly disapproving looks or uninvited lectures, all conducted with a sugar coating of sweetness.

My sewing finished, Melanie and I walked out her front door, circumventing the neighborhood baseball game taking place on her front lawn. I struggled to maintain my end of the conversation in between swallows to keep from throwing up. I mentioned how much I missed my annual trips to New York City. Flying there now would be like going on vacation only to get a bad case of the flu.

"You only live once," she said. Suddenly, Melanie erupted, her eyes hot and searing. "Anne, I've lost patience with the way you've let your health problems consume all your thoughts." I stood there paralyzed, taken aback. Tears stung my eyes. "I hope you find the strength to pull yourself together. You need to seek help to get out of this all-consuming state you're in," she said, shaking her fierce head in my direction.

I got into my car. While I backed down the driveway, Melanie called out in a syrupy, sweet voice, "But I'll always love you as a friend."

I drove home muttering to myself, "If this is love, God help us!"

Once home, staggering through the front door, I reached for the buffered vitamin C powder. Nausea washed up my throat in waves, pain split my head like an ax striking wood, the room spun as if I were on a merry-go-round. I lay on the couch, unable to move or eat dinner. Outraged as I was at Melanie, the event had also provided relief. At last she had come out and said she thought I was a hypochondriac. I would much prefer she do that than release her opinions slowly in thinly veiled remarks as she had been doing for years. In the end, it took three days to recover from 20 minutes in Melanie's basement.

MCS had a way of smoking out people's true natures like nothing I'd experienced before. When others responded to me, their underlying character tended to grow more extreme and obvious – like loud, raucous music blaring in my ears. The judgmental folks became more holier-than-thou, the compassionate ones more understanding. The need to judge others seemed a terrible affliction. I noticed people couldn't listen or learn while they were judging. My illness taught me that with the distractions of daily living, we don't know friends and acquaintances as well as we think. For instance, until MCS arrived, I had never noticed how bitter and insecure a person Melanie was or how courageous and generous Joan was. Having MCS was a little like going on trips with people I thought I knew well and learning more about them in the first two days than I'd ever learned back home during years of a relationship.

Sally Newell had a surprising observation about the event with Melanie in our next session. "I think this is really about hurt feelings," she said. My face went blank. Her theory sounded bizarre. "If you're sick all the time and a drag to be around, her feelings probably get hurt. The situation isn't unpleasant only for you. It's unpleasant for her. You don't have as much energy to put into her feelings." I looked off into the distance, trying to make sense of what Sally said. The setting sun smeared its liquid gold across the window. I shifted in my chair. All at once, I remembered how sometimes I caught myself feeling hurt when a friend with young children didn't make much effort to get together with me. Melanie herself hadn't had as much time or energy for our friendship since she began having children. But after thinking about it, I wouldn't take the feelings personally because I recognized that raising children and doing it well consumed enormous amounts of time and energy. I could see why Melanie's feelings might be hurt.

"The problem is that Melanie isn't aware enough of herself to know that her feelings are hurt," Sally continued. "With someone like that, you can't tell her that her lectures hurt your feelings. That will only trigger more of them. We don't know why this happens," she said with an upturned hand, "but statistically it does. It's something like how the more vulnerable a person looks, the more likely a violent person will attack him."

Fortunately Melanie's was the only friendship that went sour during those years. Having MCS was so hard on relationships; it's a wonder I have any friends left at all. My friends should be nominated for sainthood for all they've endured. Fortunately, most of my friends were compassionate and understanding from the beginning. Others, like my friend Lee Baker, took a while to come around. At first, when I told her about the strange health symptoms cropping up, she offered lukewarm sympathy – more out of not understanding the condition than outright skepticism.

"How annoying," Lee said lightly as we sat in her pale green living room, the translucent white curtains rippling in the breeze. I loved being in this room with its eclectic furnishings. Lee had an imaginative way of finding discarded items in salvage shops and transforming them into art objects. "But," Lee continued, "are you sure this doesn't have anything to do with your arthritis? How do you know indoor air is more polluted than outdoor air?" I explained how the symptoms had come on suddenly the first day in a new office, how at first they would disappear outside the building, how other employees had similar health troubles.

"That's a tough one," Lee responded, arms hugging her bent knees, sinking back into down-filled cushions, "because other people can get psychosomatic symptoms simply from hearing about yours."

"But most staff suffer alone," I explained. "It isn't until they compare symptoms with someone else that they hear of others with similar problems." Already I felt tired of the topic. Always having to explain myself, justify my illness. Maybe a few people have psychosomatic-related symptoms, I continued. But for every person with potentially psychosomatic problems, there are many more people denying their health troubles because they're afraid of retaliation or of losing their jobs.

As I bade goodbye, Lee said, standing on her porch, "I do hope your health will improve soon." Months later, when we met at a park, she told me, her brown eyes engaged and shining, "Anne, I've been hearing about more people with your condition." She pushed her blond hair from her eyes. "One woman at work is struggling to keep her job, but our office is making her sick. And I've read magazine articles about this sick-building syndrome phenomenon."

I nodded. "Unfortunately this problem appears to be on the rise," I said. We stood still, watching a group of ducks waddle toward the pond.

∽

The idea of disease as personal responsibility permeates both alternative and conventional healthcare, and advocates of alternative healthcare can be as self-righteous as the mainstream medicine they criticize. And they can be every bit as convinced they are right. Alternative healthcare advocates often proposed slightly different explanations for my illness, although the stress/attitude belief predominated. They often advanced the popular New Age belief that this was meant to happen to me. Fate had sent Anne Lipscomb a devastating illness for a purpose. *Maybe someday you'll understand why this happened*, people would say in confident, matter-of-fact tones. They may as well have said, *You are meant to be sick and I am supposed to be healthy*. Although some life events may occur for a larger reason, I found it impossible to presume that some karmic force was operating in my life, that I was predestined to arrive at this juncture. Even if this belief can be true, who knows if it is in every single situation? Who among us is qualified to make that judgment? In the end, the most honest conclusion I could draw is that, for whatever reason, some people are luckier with their health than others.

A few friends expressed how threatening they found my illness, since they were exposed daily to the same chemicals that made me sick. Some even began to notice they had subtle reactions to chemicals themselves. Others appeared overwhelmed to learn of a new health threat, given our society's seemingly relentless onslaught of alarming health warnings. We get frustrated when teenagers won't heed the dangers of something like cigarette smoking because they think themselves invincible. But we adults can do the same thing with evidence mounting about chemicals. When faced with information about chemicals' harmful effects, we often believe it's not going to happen to us, just as teenagers do. Or that if we don't see any obvious health damage from chemicals, then they must not be injuring us.

Early in my illness, the running moral judgment was taking a toll. Clearly I had to find ways to contend with the situation. Being a private person, it was hard to find myself so discussed and interpreted. Not having undertaken therapy with Sally yet, I scheduled an appointment with counselor Bob Chapman to talk about how to cope with other people who couldn't cope with my illness. I noticed I had become defensive, and I didn't like it.

Bob helped me see that containing the talk would help. Most people can't stand listening to another person's suffering for too long, he explained. They'll either tend to shut down, get mad, give advice, or make judgments. People generally react in the same way that their parents reacted to their feelings and suffering as children. Try to see through them and how little they know what they're talking about. Bob noted that people think they're giving you great advice but really they're anxious because they feel the need to fix your problem. Containing the talk would be infinitely more effective than explaining my point of view to others, hoping they would listen and understand. He suggested I be selective about who I shared my experience with. Loneliness might be better than the anguish of expression.

After the appointment, I began editing myself when people asked how I was doing. Even with Ted, who had days when he doubted that my health problems were as severe as I said they were. Those who fully accepted my illness received a free and open answer; others got the most conservative estimate of what I thought they could hear without triggering their judgments. Months later, life felt significantly more relaxed. The moral judgments had dropped precipitously – except from the bureaucrats, medical examiners, and Melanie. Perhaps keeping my illness to myself made me feel more alone, but I definitely felt calmer.

Curiously, as my health improved and I shared less of my illness, people began treating me better. The difference was dramatic. If others noticed I was happier, it was not only because health therapies were working. I simply encountered less blame and skepticism. Now some people even began complimenting me on my great attitude, the same attitude I'd had all along.

My mother called one day to ask me for help. "We're building new offices at work," she said, "and I want to make sure they are healthy for our staff." She was on the board of directors at an environmental conservation group. "I would just hate to think of something like what's happened to you and other District employees occur in our office. Besides, in our business, we're the last people who should have these kinds of problems." We talked about my writing a letter summarizing what I'd learned. "Please send me a copy of it," my mother asked, "because

I want to follow up – make sure that they're taking these issues into consideration." I hung up thinking about what a difference it could have made if one of the District's board of directors or higher-ups had shown such authentic commitment.

☙

After so many years of living with a long-term illness, I've concluded there are certain ways I'd like to be treated by friends and family. First, I appreciate it immensely when a friend can listen to me share my health troubles without judging me, dismissing my feelings, giving unasked-for advice or engaging in "Things could be worse because you could have a fatal disease" talk. This simple but difficult gesture lightens my burden considerably, at least for a while. When I discuss my long-term illness that has no cure, it's natural for others to feel pressured to fix my problem or to want to say something profound that will make me feel better. Even I occasionally struggle with these urges around my friends with chronic sicknesses. I've found it helps me the most when a friend simply accepts that she doesn't understand my illness and its accompanying challenges, rather than assume that she grasps it enough to throw out unasked-for suggestions. The well-intentioned suggestions are seldom useful and they also remind me of how little others understand my sickness, which can make me feel even lonelier. If my health troubles make a friend feel pressured to solve my problems, I love it when, instead of making suggestions, she says: "Is there anything I can do to help or support you?" If a friend wants to share a health remedy she thinks could help me, I prefer it if she says: "I know of a remedy that might improve your illness. Let me know if you ever want to hear about it." Because my sickness makes me a magnet for relentless health suggestions, and after years of experience with it, I am my best expert at knowing what works and when to try new things.

Secondly, I so appreciate it when friends are flexible around my health troubles and don't get offended if, for instance, I mention that something they're wearing sickens me. It takes patience and understanding because it may take us a while to figure out what the offending substance is. Sometimes when I raise the topic, I fear that others might think me controlling. But really, I'm just trying to find ways to enjoy a friend's company. At my sickest, some incredibly understanding people have even changed into one of my old sweatsuits while visiting my home, because the scent of laundry products in their clothes was making me ill. Since laundry products can be highly fragrant, I, along with other friends with MCS, must stay indoors while nearby neighbors wash and dry their clothes. I would find it a welcome and extraordinary act of generosity were my neighbors to ask me if their laundry products bothered me and, if so, if there were any unscented ones they could use instead. I don't expect them to do this, but such a gesture would help improve the quality of my life.

My illness can confuse others, and perhaps even seem unbelievable at times, because I may be able to go to a friend's house easily one day but the next week land in bed for a day after being in the same home. My tolerance for chemicals can vary wildly by the day, and it can plummet because of things like hormonal fluctuations, seasonal allergies, or a cold. The particular environment I'm in also affects my sensitivities. I might be able to tolerate sitting in a meeting with a group of people because the room has a good ventilation system but the next day be sickened by one person in my living room who dries her clothes with dryer sheets. Even within the MCS community, we each react to different things and some are more sensitive than others; and it can sometimes be hard for us to accept the differences.

Lastly, another way I'd like to be treated involves my participation as well. With a long-term illness, sometimes I find it useful to discuss and set boundaries within a relationship, to prevent friends from getting burned out by my health troubles or from wanting to distance themselves from me. Sometimes I set my own boundaries, like deciding I won't discuss my health struggles with a friend for more than 10 minutes, and then I'll move on to other topics or ask her how she's been doing. Around friends with whom I share my health troubles, I might even preface my thoughts by saying: "I'd like to talk a little about my illness. I'm not expecting you to fix things or to come up with advice. Are you in the mood, or should we do this another time?" Likewise, I would welcome a friend telling me what her limits are, for example, that she's had a stressful day and while she cares about what I'm going through, she'd prefer to discuss my ailments the next day. In a way, I would feel relieved that she could feel comfortable being that honest with me.

♋

For many years I lived with the delusion that with time, people in my life would develop a good understanding of what I go through with my illness and the enormity of what I'm up against. But years passed without it happening, and I slowly realized that it was unrealistic, even unfair, of me to expect others to grasp it. Because unless someone has personally experienced a major, severely disruptive and little-understood sickness that confines her to home for 15 years, she can only learn about my illness intellectually, which is inherently a very limited form of knowledge.

My closest friends, who have been around my sickness for 16 years, grasp only about 20 percent of my illness experience. A few of them, who have personally suffered from long-term sicknesses, understand more than that. But I do not have any friends who have been so sick that they have been forced to live housebound for over a decade. Ironically, as the years pass, many people in my life seem to grasp less and less of my sickness – not only because at this point I share little of it with them, but also because I've become more skilled at living well despite the illness. The better I get at managing my illness, the easier and less serious it seems to look to others. It's something like how easy playing tennis looks when you're watching a professional tennis player during a game and you've never played the sport yourself.

I have friends with long-term illnesses whose spouses have lived around their sicknesses for more than a decade. Their partners are sympathetic and supportive and want to understand what my sick friends endure, yet they still don't fully grasp what it is like to struggle daily with a long-term illness. They can't understand how much harder it is to cope with a sickness that may never end and the anguish one can feel when healthcare providers can't help much. If I were a healthy person in the same situation, I wouldn't be able to do it either. Nevertheless, partners and friends can still have compassion, which helps more than words can express, and they can develop some empathy and understanding by listening to the stories of ill people with an open heart and mind.

141

In moments when I feel especially lonely, because something as monumental and painful as my illness is so little seen by others, it helps me to try to accept that life and the human condition can sometimes be a lonely experience, even for the healthy. But my illness takes me to an even lonelier place. For me, one of the worst consequences of my sickness is that not only has it been hard for me to live with the illness for 16 years, but it has been a drag for my friends to be around it as well. When my illness becomes exacerbated enough that it is noticeable to others, some friends seem not to be as interested in being in touch with me. During those difficult times, I find it helpful to redouble my efforts to be upbeat around others and to focus upon aspects of my life that bring me joy and pleasure.

Ultimately, learning skills that helped me maintain relationships with a long-term illness, and even make new friends, transformed my frustration enough that my illness revealed to me the power of love – and not just emotional love. Years after the onslaught of MCS, when most people had accepted that my condition was serious, I became aware of a physical presence surrounding Ted and me. The presence was subtle but palpable. It was something I sensed – the way you feel someone noiselessly come into the room behind you while sitting at a desk. You can't see or hear the person, but you sense someone is there. I probably wouldn't have noticed it had I not spent years leading a quiet, reflective existence, or had I not become attuned to something as intangible as the moving vibration acupuncturists call *chi*.

The presence felt something like a golden cocoon enveloping me. It was as if the love and concern of friends, family and healthcare providers had transformed into something creative and constructive. I concluded that we are all sources of energy or spirit, both positive and negative, but the greatest of these is love. In my lowest moments, tuning into this golden cocoon of support helped to lift my sagging spirits. It helped hold me up when I couldn't do it alone. I came to believe that genuine love and help from others during a serious illness can literally help one become the person one does.

After I saw people's attitudes toward me change, and when I saw people grow, my anger melted away. I knew I might have been as skeptical

142

standing in their shoes. MCS certainly humbled me. In time, I came to believe that experts and institutions would also change after many years and overwhelming evidence had piled up or when the tide couldn't be held back any longer.

In the meantime, I still had to trudge through the trenches with the District and the workers' compensation system. The District's position hadn't changed a bit. Since the District was challenging my claim, the Board of Industrial Insurance Appeals would decide my case. A hearing, similar to a trial, would be scheduled, but I didn't know when. I was trying to find a lawyer but I was discovering no one wanted to take on a case as murky as one involving sick-building syndrome and multiple chemical sensitivity. Only a handful of people in the entire state, I learned, had won a case like mine. Without a good lawyer, I worried I wouldn't stand much of a chance.

A Simple Twist of Fate

I suppose I should have seen it coming. One day, out of nowhere, my boss Nancy sent me a letter. Dread washed over me when I opened the paper. Receiving mail from the District was about as welcome as a root canal. My year's leave of absence was about to end, she reminded me. My doctor had to send in a statement about whether I could return to work. The letter took me by surprise since I had just talked to Nancy by telephone the day before and she hadn't mentioned anything.

My doctor promptly faxed in a reply stating that I could begin working two hours a day from my home, increasing my hours as health permitted and occasionally attending meetings in buildings other than the District's new offices. Nancy would be open to the proposal, I hoped, since with a recent reorganization she was asking staff to consider working part-time, and to take on writing assignments that had been handled by outside contractors for years. In addition, to help reduce traffic on Seattle's congested roads and to conserve energy, the District had been encouraging employees to work partially from home or other sites.

Meanwhile, downtown at the District, years after moving to new offices, employees' health problems continued, but complaints about air quality had faded away. Health problems hadn't disappeared; they had just gone underground. Staff had gotten the message that if they spoke up they wouldn't get anywhere, and they might risk being perceived as problem employees. It was clear the emphasis would be on keeping the peace.

Around this time staff were particularly nervous about job security as the District was in the midst of one of its perennial reorganizations: Departments were being restructured, work responsibilities shifted, staff laid off. As part of this downsizing, committees met to draw up a number of District principles such as "We act with integrity," "We treat each other with trust and respect," and "We live the Guiding Principles." These goals were written down in places like notepads and computer mouse pads.

Each manager considered my case from his or her own department's needs. Communications Director Nancy Murdoch had an absent employee whose work needed to get done; the Facilities Department wanted to protect the building's image and contain financial costs; the workers' compensation group had to keep employee claims as low as possible to keep costs down; and the Legal and Personnel Departments were concerned about liability and setting legal precedent. No matter what department or perspective, my case and others were still no closer to resolution.

Within several hours of receiving my doctor's proposal, Nancy mailed me a letter firing me. The news shocked me like a bolt of lightning, more so because Nancy didn't call me herself. I felt as if I were a piece of furniture that had been thrown out on the sidewalk – that I was valuable only as long as I was useful. But I had given the District my best work for eight years and was a human being who deserved to be treated with dignity and, thanks to the District, I now had a disability that left me with exorbitant bills.

Probably, I surmised, Nancy thought she had done all she could just as the District said it had done enough to respond to air quality problems. The District had still not made any significant improvements to the building's air quality, such as overhauling the ventilation system, nor had it done simple things like reviewing the products used to clean the office and replacing them with natural or low-chemical ones. Somehow management's standards for treating employees seemed far lower than what they expected from them. But I didn't think Nancy would have made the decision alone. Most likely, the Legal and Personnel Departments would have also been in on it. From the beginning when

I reported my health symptoms, to the day I was fired, the conduct of most of the involved District staff, in my opinion, lacked professional integrity. It would be years before I would fully realize the disastrous effect such an absence of integrity had had on my health and that not all employers responded to work-related illnesses this way.

Then the air quality situation took a new turn. Joan – tired of the "let's keep a lid on it" approach – went straight to the president of the District. She told him of the extent of employee health problems, described the experts' limited checks of the premises and the so-called "independent" medical exams, and how a proposed employee questionnaire had been rejected, and she informed him that I'd been fired. The District president was genuinely surprised. He knew me well because over the years I had produced many events and projects in which he had been personally involved. The president assumed the problem had disappeared. In fact, it had been more than two years since anyone had told him about air quality problems. Right away the president told Joan he would ask a District lawyer and a department director to look into the situation and report back to him. Several days later he even dropped by Joan's office to inquire about how the air was that day.

I took in the news cautiously. Would this be the twist I had been waiting for? Was this the thing that would finally push the air quality issue out into the great wide open and toward resolution? Perhaps the letter was the beginning that would strangely move everything to its fate? However things might turn out, I thought they were held in hands other than mine, that the answer would not be something I could control. But was fate the right way to think about what I had been going through? I wasn't sure. My mind paused on this, and wandered to another land.

❧

The phrase "everything is in the hand of heaven" returned to me all of a sudden, and with it a poignant memory of acceptance and fate. You see, growing up in Egypt, my days were steeped in a world where everything was believed to be in the hand of heaven. Do your duty and leave the rest up to God, the Egyptians would say. Or, I'll see you Thursday, *in-sha-allah*, "if God is willing." Or if you asked someone how he was doing he'd say fine, *el-ham-di-la-la*, "thanks be to God." This was such a stark contrast to our American tendency toward seeing most everything as being under our control. Of course, we can't always control everything, as much as we think we do. Sometimes when people accept a problem as their fate, they may actually be able to solve it, or at least to bring about an improvement. The key is being able to discern the difference in any given situation. But for the Egyptians, seeing things as being in the hand of heaven helped them be calmer and more accepting of what came their way.

Shortly after moving into our villa, hearing the doorbell chime, I opened our towering glass-and-wrought-iron door to find Mr. and Mrs. El Hamid beaming down at me, a rolled-up prayer rug tucked under Mr. El Hamid's arm. He had just returned from the mosque. They introduced themselves as our next-door neighbors. Mrs. El Hamid was a thickset woman with black hair tied back in a bun and warm, crinkly eyes. Her husband had a shiny dome of a head edged with black hair and a dark spot in the middle of his forehead. *El-zebiba*, the raisin, Egyptians called it. Many Muslim men had such a bruise from touching their head to the floor five times a day in prayer. The El Hamids had heard my mother was ill. Could they come in and pray for her good health? Sure, I said. Thinking nothing of it, I led them upstairs to my parents' bedroom. We burst through the door to find my stunned mother springing out of bed, searching for her bathrobe in a frenzy. But she still had time to give me the look — the look that let me know I was in trouble but that we wouldn't get around to it until our company left.

Ahlan wusahlan, "Welcome to Egypt," Mr. El Hamid said, smiling with his whole body. Mrs. El Hamid placed a wrapped package tied with a white ribbon in my mother's lap. Her husband asked if he could say prayers at the foot of the bed. Mom looked startled, as if she was trying to rise to the occasion, but she murmured, "Yes, how kind of you." Before saying prayers, Mr. El Hamid explained, he had to wash his hands and feet. I led him to the bathroom as my mother opened her gift. Petals of tissue paper fell away to reveal a pink beaded purse that Mrs. El Hamid had made herself. My mother held it up, oohing and aahing, and she thanked Mrs. El Hamid profusely.

"How have you found your time in Egypt so far?" Mrs. El Hamid sat back in her chair.

"We are enjoying ourselves immensely," Mom said, smoothing the covers around her, as if meeting new neighbors while lying in bed was the most natural thing in the world. "But there is so much to do. The children start school next week – Annie in first grade and Billy in kindergarten. And I have to hire servants." Mom ran a hand through her hair and leaned back against the pillows. "The first week here, when we lived in the Nile Hilton hotel, we especially loved going on a *felucca* ride down the Nile. Seeing the sun set behind the distant pyramids of Giza was breathtaking."

Meanwhile, Mr. El Hamid quietly placed his small Oriental carpet on the floor, the end with the pointed design facing Mecca in the east. I hung back in the shadowed corner of the room, not wanting to miss out on the action. This was the most exciting thing to happen all day. Even though it was hot outside, our villa's thick stucco walls and half-closed shutters cooled the room. Carefully, Mr. El Hamid lowered himself to the floor, folding his legs underneath him, and sat back on his feet. He lowered his body to the ground. Slices of light fell over his back like a soft spotlight. His lips moved continuously but silently. My mother looked fascinated as she watched him, his outstretched arms up in the air, then down on the floor, murmuring prayers the whole while. Eventually, watching people pray this way would come to seem normal, and when my nanny bent down on her prayer rug throughout the day, I would instinctually know not to disturb her. My legs grew tired, but I couldn't move while Mr. El Hamid was still praying. At last he rose from his rug. Smiling, Mr. El Hamid and his wife bent over Mom, shook her hand warmly, and talked about how glad they were to have us as their new neighbors. Mom thanked them again for coming and for praying for her health.

One Final Trial

I glanced at the clock. It was 10 in the morning. At the front of a bleak, windowless room, my friend Mary Cummings raised her right hand and swore to tell the truth, the whole truth, and nothing but the truth, so help her God. At last the time had come to try my workers' compensation case. My lawyer, Chuck Kimbrough, sat behind a long, narrow table with his legal assistant, scribbling notes. At the other end of the table sat the district lawyer, Jim Hazan. Mountainous stacks of paper and folders lay before both men. Across from them, at the front of the room, Mary spoke clearly into a table-top microphone while a court reporter recorded her words. Off to the side, a woman filmed the event on a video camera. I was presenting my case to the Board of Industrial Insurance Appeals, a separate entity from the Department of Labor & Industries. When a worker wasn't satisfied with a decision rendered by the Department of Labor & Industries, an appeal to this board was the next place to seek a different outcome.

On this day of trial, four-and-a-half years had passed since I had first become ill. There were times when I despaired this day would never come, times when I had wanted to give up the fight. To be here, I had to wear my mask. As it was, I would hear only Mary's testimony in person, to get a sense of the process, and the rest of the hearing I'd watch by video at home because being here all day, in an old, musty building, would be too hard on my health. Out of respect for my chemical sensitivities, all staff at the appeals office had been asked not to wear fragrances, even deodorant, during the course of my hearing.

At last I had found a lawyer, and an excellent one at that. Adeline Crinks of On the Job Injuries had highly recommended him when the District continued to fight my claim so hard that I had no options left but to argue my case at an L&I hearing. At first Chuck Kimbrough had declined to take my case because he had no experience with the workers' compensation system. Chuck had offered to call other lawyers to see if they would take me on. What he learned was discouraging. No attorneys who were experienced with chemical-related illnesses would take on another client. The success rate was just too dismal.

Chuck enjoyed practicing law because he had loved public speaking and debating since junior high school, and he liked people and problem-solving. But he had never specifically set out to be a lawyer. During Chuck's sophomore year of college, a friend who had been Chuck's next-door neighbor, said he planned to go to law school. Chuck thought about the idea and discussed it with his father, who liked the idea and knew it was a way for Chuck to advance himself. Chuck's father had gone to trade school himself, because his own father had died during his childhood, and afterward he'd served in the Army training young men in machinery during World War II, and later worked as an insurance claims adjuster. When the boys took the test, which today is called the LSAT, both received good scores. But Chuck forgot about the idea until the end of his junior year, when his friend asked him if he would go with him to law school. Somehow Chuck decided to go, and once there, he didn't want to fail.

By some stroke of luck, in the end Chuck decided to take my case. He would have to get legal advice from a colleague experienced with workers' compensation, he explained. I felt relieved. I knew Chuck had an excellent reputation. One lawyer had told me they didn't make lawyers any finer than him. Nevertheless, I was worried. My chance of winning compensation was already low, even with the most experienced attorney. Only a handful of workers in Washington State had won compensation for an illness related to sick-building syndrome. With a glimmer of hope in my heart, and a spark of resolve in my eyes, I was trying to beat the odds.

Mary Cummings offered to testify. She had been my close friend for almost 20 years; in fact, she was the first person I had met in Seattle. Weeks after graduating from college, before I had set out for Washington state, a family friend had called me to say he had a niece living in Seattle. He had already called her and told her about me and she had generously offered to put me up for the first few weeks. That is how I had the great fortune of meeting Mary and her family. I would be the houseguest who came for two weeks and stayed on and off for six years, her family would joke, but that's how well we got along. Chuck began by asking Mary to describe our relationship, the range of activities I had been engaged in before moving to the new District building, and my emotional makeup.

Mary characterized me as one of the most energetic and organized people she had ever met and recalled once finding me napping on the living room couch a half-hour before a 12-person dinner party. She testified that I was a reflective person with a deep, meditative side, and that I had a good sense of humor. Although my intellectual capacity had remained throughout my illness, Mary found it diminished because of my low energy. In response to Chuck's questions about my weight changes, Mary described me as skeletal and emaciated, compared to before, and she noted how my activity level had dropped to almost nothing and that my conversation seemed drawn out and strained. She admitted that she saw me down at moments, but said she found me resilient and optimistic given the restrictions of my life. Mary ended by discussing how I had painted six rooms in her home with oil-based paints 10 years before developing multiple chemical sensitivity, and that I didn't have any adverse health effects from it.

Next, District-hired lawyer Jim Hazan looked up from his notes to begin his cross-examination. He didn't look anything like I thought he would. He was a slim man with tanned skin the color of a polished hazelnut and perfectly-blown-dry-blond hair. But his eyes struck me the most – so empty and flat and haunting, as if no one were home. When Jason had introduced me to Jim, the District attorney's eyes had darted about the room as he held out a limp hand, which slipped out of my handshake like a dead fish. He was about as personable as a turnip. I shivered at the man's seeming callousness, at his ability to affect my entire financial future. To inject much-needed humor into the situation, I privately decided to nickname him Jim the Bottom Feeder.

Chuck told me it saddened him that the District hired Jim so early in the process of evaluating my claim. Jim was one of the top lawyers in Seattle, who specialized in helping employers defeat workers' compensation claims. The system wasn't supposed to work like this, Chuck said, shaking his head.

Jim Hazan cross-examined Mary in a soft, monotone voice. Did she know the specific dates when my arthritis was diagnosed or what medications I took? Had she read my medical file? Did she ever attend medical school or have any psychiatric training? Unlike jury trials, this case would be presented to technocrats who were more impressed by such technical evidence. The District's strategy was becoming clear in his line of questioning.

I greeted Mary afterward and thanked her for her testimony. Just having her there supporting me helped lighten my mood. I had been waging this battle all by myself for far too long, and it was a welcome relief to have a fellow combatant fighting alongside me, even if hers was a limited role. We walked out together discussing the morning's events while Mary made jokes about the District lawyer. Someone needs to muss up his hair, she said, a grin the size of California on her face. I laughed, perhaps louder than usual, needing at this moment something like Mary's wonderful sense of humor to loosen me up.

Several of my former District colleagues waved to us from the reception area, where they waited to testify. Joan and Molly joined us, and we huddled together to talk in hushed voices about Jim Hazan's cross-examination. They had met Mary earlier in the morning and already the three seemed like old friends as Joan and Molly joked and hugged Mary goodbye. We were a clan of women united behind a common cause. The women's spirited defense on my behalf shored me up like a lifeboat sent out to reel in people from a capsized ship. Lord knows, I desperately needed them for emotional support as well as for their testimony because my nerves were stretched taut like a frightened animal's at the sound of thunder. Nothing had prepared me for how excruciatingly difficult this hearing would be, listening to accounts of the ravages of my sickness and to Jim's repeated attempts to discredit me, though Chuck had tried to warn me. If the battle ever gets so hard that it damages your health, he told me, I'll understand if you want to quit the case. Coping with my illness and the independent medical exams had been tribulation enough, now the hearing turned up the heat many degrees and scorched me with its intensity and negativity. Part of me felt incredulous that lawsuits were so common because so far I had found the process to be extraordinarily stressful and time-consuming.

Chuck had also warned me that the more I could help him, the better my chances were of winning, but I had failed to grasp the enormity of the task. I had no idea what I was in for. Chuck was forever asking me to dig up information or to draft documents, as if I was his assistant, and it could take me days to fulfill each request. In the early years, Ted had said he would help me with the case, especially since he was adamant that I pursue compensation. But I ended up having to do almost all of the work myself because I was the only one who knew all the various pieces of information. Unfortunately, most of it simply could not be delegated. A friend who had worked for a workers' compensation system once told me some injured workers who had filed injury claims developed a second illness due to the stress of the process. Between this hearing and the independent medical exams, I was beginning to understand why.

Next Joan was sworn in. At Chuck's prompting, she recounted how excited our Communications Department felt about moving to the new building as well as the physical symptoms she experienced in the new office – her nosebleeds, headaches, ringing ears, difficulty concentrating – and how she and I knew of 60 employees also suffering from building-related health problems. Joan explained that, years after moving, she began to feel as if she had the flu upon arriving at work, that the air in her office felt heavy and stagnant, and how she had decided to investigate by climbing up on top of her office cabinets to place her hand against the ceiling air vent. No air was coming out, the same problem we'd had the first year in the office. Apparently the ventilation system was designed to automatically shut off when her office reached a certain temperature so there would be no air flow for a time. Joan solved the problem by stringing a strand of raffia through the ventilation grate so that when it stopped bobbing about, she knew to call the Facilities Department to ask them to turn the air flow back on.

During cross-examination, Jim Hazan used the same kind of questions he had had for Mary. As Joan answered each question in a calm, measured voice, I silently hoped the District managers wouldn't retaliate against her. Joan had been subpoenaed, so technically she did not have a choice about testifying. But Joan answered everything honestly and emphatically without dodging a single question. If she had been anxious to please the District, she could have been more evasive.

What a colossal waste of human potential, I thought, so much time and money spent by both sides. If we had, instead, applied the same effort to solving the air quality problems in the District's new building, think of where we might be. The $10,000 I had spent so far on legal expenses made me nervous. Even though Chuck would be paid a fee only if we won, I still had to fork up money for things like medical witnesses and the videographer. The bills rose each day like a flooded river. Was I gambling away valuable savings? Before, when I had felt apprehensive about legal costs, I had always come back to the same conclusion. I was making a small contribution toward getting sick-building syndrome recognized, even if I lost, by being one more person rattling the cage of those too powerful to show us their faces. All too frequently, I concluded, the only language the higher-ups at the District understood was the bottom line. When enough money had been paid out in claims for sick-building syndrome, I thought, change was more likely to follow.

To prepare for my doctor's testimony, Chuck had asked me to read my medical chart notes. All 450 pages of them. The notes would familiarize me with material doctors on both sides would be using. If any witness left out information that would be important to my legal case, I was to let Chuck know and he could adjust his questions accordingly.

Reading my chart notes had turned out to be a disturbing experience, to say the least. I could see how adversaries might deduce from my medical notes that I was merely a hypochondriac. My file documented a slew of physical symptoms, most of them not verifiable on standard medical tests. Also, since physicians don't write notes with a patient's future legal case in mind, the notes were often easy to manipulate and there were holes in my chart. A stranger reading it wouldn't realize that some of my symptoms eventually improved – like how the stuffiness in my head disappeared when a dust-mite allergy was diagnosed. It just looked like all of my problems continued unabated. Adding to the problem, when I went to doctors, with appointments so brief, I focused on solving problems, not on talking about what was working well in my life. Thus the notes didn't reflect the whole picture – that I was having modest success with my health therapies. By not recording improvements, the notes could unintentionally make me look like a clueless patient who kept pursuing health therapies even though they weren't producing results.

If my medical chart sometimes omitted important information, at other times it was completely inaccurate. My favorite error was the section where a doctor wrote that I was drinking my urine as part of an alternative healthcare therapy. Unfortunately, I was dismayed to discover, once medical notes got into a file, most people assumed they were true, the way that we assume news articles are true once they're in print. My chart grew even more distorted, if that was possible, when a subsequent specialist reviewed the erroneous notes about drinking my urine and wrote that I was eating my feces. Once the shock of reading this had worn off, I shook with laughter. Truth could be stranger than fiction, indeed. In the heat of preparing for the hearing, neither Chuck nor I had noticed a chart note that explained the error. Years before, when I'd had terrible trouble eating, one physician had asked me to keep a diary of how much I was eating and how much urine my body was producing. The urine list was on the same page as the food list, although they were in separate columns.

Dr. William Sherwood, my arthritis doctor for more than 10 years, was the first physician to testify. Chuck asked him to describe his medical practice, his teaching position at the University of Washington medical school, his professional memberships. He reviewed my medical file with Dr. Sherwood, as well as medications prescribed through the years, then asked him about his experience with me.

Dr. Sherwood replied that he found me to be a rational, steady person who, although occasionally depressed by my problems, was not primarily a depressed person. There was nothing about me that was psychosomatic, he believed, and in the past when I'd had symptoms that others thought were psychosomatic, these had turned out to be real conditions.

There are internal debates, Chuck continued, in both legal and medical communities about what is *subjective* and what is *objective*. Could you give us an overview, in terms of objective identifiers, that she has a form of arthritis known as spondylitis?

Dr. Sherwood nodded. "First, I'd like to comment on what is objective versus what is subjective. Most of what we do as physicians is based on subjective evidence, that is, the patient will tell us something is wrong. If I've known a patient for years and he comes in with chest pain – saying it's as if there's an elephant on his chest – right away I say, "This could be a heart attack." I don't say, "Come back when you've got some objective evidence, like when I can see your heart bulge." When Anne initially presented with a form of arthritis called spondylitis, we found no objective evidence, just an excellent history of inflammatory disease. Eventually she had x-ray changes in joints in her back that demonstrated she had spondylitis."

Dr. Sherwood then stated his opinion that exposure to chemicals in the District building had aggravated my spondylitis and fibromyalgia. He based his opinion on the fact that he'd known me a long time and that prior to the move, I had an active, functioning life and that it abruptly changed once I was in the new office. Chuck asked him about the methodology the physician had used.

"We don't deal with 90 percent certainties in most of medicine," Dr. Sherwood replied. "We deal with 50 or 52 percent, like we do with law. The best example I can give is that everybody now knows anti-inflammatories like aspirin can cause ulcers. How do we know that? We know it based on case reports and probability. We don't base it on 90 percent proof. If we based medicine on 90 percent proof, we would be doing nothing for anyone."

This was a powerful moment. Surely this could reply to all those who demanded empirical proof for every illness, for every chemical contamination. Dr. Sherwood was a fair and reasoned voice here.

By the third day of the hearing, we were way behind schedule. Environmental medicine physician Dr. Cunningham and Dr. Osborne, my primary care doctor, had also testified that they believed something in the new District building had aggravated my health. Other witnesses, like my former supervisors, had their testimony rescheduled for the following week.

I arrived to have lunch with Chuck and his legal assistant. With the hearing running overtime and my testimony scheduled immediately after lunch, we had only 20 minutes to eat our food. The three of us sat at a sidewalk café, beneath green-and-white-striped umbrellas, music blaring from a pair of loudspeakers. I asked Chuck questions through my face mask, trying to get a sense of how he thought things were going. Chuck talked about what a circus the hearing had been so far and how, together with the layers of bureaucracy involved, it didn't make economic sense for a lawyer to take on Labor & Industry cases because it took too long to prove the case, especially with an illness like MCS.

The District lawyer had a very calculated strategy, Chuck explained. He didn't want me to have a psychiatric condition because I could actually get a disability award for that. Instead, he tried to create a gray area – to imply I was a hypochondriac, but not officially diagnose me with it – so I didn't have enough proof linking my health problems to exposure to chemicals in the District building.

Driving home that day, part of me wanted to curl up in a fetal position, to wash away the stains from this stressful week; but another part of me couldn't help but think about it all over and over again. I thought about how hard it had been to listen to witnesses catalogue the losses in my life set in motion by exposures in the District building. Rarely did I think about my losses all at once like that or tally them up in this way. It was too much to absorb in one sitting. I thought about the person I once had been and the life I had taken for granted. I thought about what a completely different world it was for those who were healthy and how much you have to change coming from the perspective of illness.

I thought about my fragile energy and how, if I lost my case, everything might have been squandered on trying to get compensation. I thought about how easy it was to manipulate a medical chart, and the realization chilled me like a freezing snow. Someone like Jim Hazan, if given the right material and the time to dig through charts, could make even Mother Teresa look bad. Lawyers are skilled at what they do, for better and for worse. I thought about what remarkable friends and healthcare providers I had, and how hard the hearing must have been on them as well.

As I pulled into my driveway, I came to the sad realization that too often in the hearing, getting to the truth wasn't the point, it was all about winning. This final thought made me feel emptied and weary.

That evening, Mary Cummings called. "Annie, I don't know how you've stood it for nearly five years. After testifying, I went home and ate way too big a lunch. I was steaming. I don't even know what I ate. Then I had to lie down and take a nap. I'm still angry about the District's lawyer and his line of questioning." She was fired up. I sat there feeling sad to have had to drag Mary into the saga, but a tinge of relief hovered at the edge of my thoughts. Her reaction showed me that the battle would be deeply upsetting for anyone, even for a person whose financial future didn't depend on the hearing's outcome. It wasn't just me. Others needed to be aware of the kinds of things like this that go on, of the personal trials, yes, but also the bureaucratic and legal ones that keep so many powerless. The story needed to be told. The fight, even if lost in some financial sense, needed to be waged.

One after the other, the remaining witnesses finished up the following week. My nerves felt frayed, like loose and hot electrical wires, while we awaited the verdict. Was I going to get help to pay my mounting healthcare bills? Was all the stress and hard work going to pay off? I didn't have to wait very long.

Chuck called to say the District was willing to settle, that I would receive workers' compensation based on my aggravated spondylitis and fibromyalgia, but not based on the MCS. The District didn't want to have to face a decision that would say I was made ill by chemicals in the building, so they thought it best to avoid this with a settlement. Ultimately, Chuck thought, I could have won such a case if they had not ended it. He explained that I had won because I had excellent testimony from traditional, mainstream doctors and because my friends not only were articulate and intuitive witnesses, but that their caring and loyalty toward me had definitely come across. In the end, the District lawyer just couldn't explain the abrupt leap of how I went from being a highly functioning employee to being so sick and disabled. He could not rationally explain the immediate onset of my chemical illness, so he and the District took what they felt was the easier path: paying out a small settlement.

I sank back into the sofa cushions in relief, tears forming in the corners of my eyes. I realized I had also won because I had an excellent lawyer, and I marveled at my luck that he had taken me on. Still, it was going to take time for the news to sink in fully. This marked the end of a four-and-a-half-year battle, a fight that had turned out to be far bloodier, far stressful, than anything I could have imagined.

I finally burst open with gratitude, like a melon splitting its tougher skin with its sweetness inside – not just for the settlement, but for living in a country that protected my free speech and my right to pursue a course of justice. It wasn't a perfect system, but it worked in this case. Most other workers, who were just as sick as me from chemical-related illnesses, had not won their cases. Only one other District employee pursued workers' compensation to the hearing stage, and despite the fact that she used my lawyer and was as sick as I was, she did not win. Nevertheless, I had been allowed to disagree with the District, to state my case without risk of harm. In America, free speech didn't just live, I thought. Free speech was a lifeblood. And it helped create a healthy foundation from which to openly discuss and solve problems, to achieve our potential as individuals and as a country. To solve sick-building syndrome, I mused, the freer and more open the dialogue was allowed, the better off we will all be in the future.

The downside was that my free speech had come with a steep price. My legal bills had mounted to more than $75,000 because the District had fought so hard. Chuck told me the District must have spent at least as much money as I had. Unlike jury trials, he explained, where the winner is awarded legal fees, I wouldn't be compensated for the legal fees and expenses. It would be deducted from my settlement. This was simply a price to be paid at the end of it all.

PART III

HEALING

The Unexpected Spiritual Journey

The Sufis, a mystic Moslem sect, say there are three ways to understand fire: You can hear about it; you can see it; or you can get burned by it. I hold this to be a way of thinking about my illness experience. Sick-building syndrome certainly threw me headlong into a roaring fire, but its searing flames taught me some of the greatest lessons of my life, lessons I might not have learned from the constant comfort of a healthy life. Knowledge gained through my head, by seeing or hearing about something, was one thing; but knowledge burned into every fiber of my being was quite another. This was more than a bodily knowledge. It wasn't just a lesson in how to live with a major illness. It was something more comprehensive, a deeper form of knowing and being.

It certainly has been one of the worst times of my life, but in many ways it also has been the most extraordinary. This is because the illness sparked within me a spiritual journey, ultimately a close relationship with my soul, which has forever enriched my life.

This was a gift. I can't take much credit for it. The illness created the fertile ground, rich in nutrient possibility. To survive the experience, and even to thrive despite everything, I wanted to find the seeds of opportunity within the crisis and nurture them into full growth. For some reason, the tendency to find hope buried in the darkest ground has been a part of my character since I was a child. It doesn't make me a better person or even right necessarily, but I feel I was born with some of this fire already in me. It's something that has brightened in me because of the illness and is something I want to share now.

I don't think we adequately appreciate what different constitutional types all of us have and how that deeply affects our character. Some Asian healthcare systems I've explored recognize and honor such differences, but for the most part we often overlook them. Ayurveda medicine practitioners, for example, believe that people with various physiologies are more prone toward certain tendencies – for instance, they believe one constitutional type leans toward anxiety, others toward characteristics like irritability, lethargy, or jealousy. In the United States, we gravitate toward seeing bodies as if they're all the same and assume people are blank slates, equally capable of achieving what they want if they just set their minds to it. There is perhaps some hopeful truth in this, but if a person has an addictive constitution, I believe he will probably struggle with compulsiveness around something like alcohol or food more than I would because I don't have an addictive physiology. Likewise, others with sturdy and stable constitutions can often take their health for granted or even abuse their bodies more than I might because they don't have this extraordinarily sensitive physiology that I've been dealt. We are all given a hand to play, a character to explore and grow.

The conditions that made MCS so difficult – the extreme isolation, the relentless physical pain, and the hostile skepticism brought about by the condition's invisibility on the medical radar – were the same factors that laid the foundation within me for rich inner growth. They forced me to a place deep within myself, where I couldn't escape or be distracted. The experience has thrown my life into sharp relief so I can better see what parts of me need changing, and in the process I can become my best self.

I certainly don't want to sentimentalize sickness as merely an experience of enlightenment. So many suffer in this world in silence and isolation. It is hard to justify or redeem much of the pain we witness. MCS unleashed a chaotic wind through my life, and in its wake a trail of unimaginable losses. Time often passed in a blur, with all my resources directed toward just getting by. A hopeful perspective doesn't automatically compensate you for your losses. Nor does illness always stimulate spiritual growth. You cannot blame anyone for being overwhelmed or seriously depressed by an illness as turbulent as MCS.

So many come to live in poverty after losing their jobs, some even have to live out of their cars because they can't find or afford housing that doesn't sicken them. Others struggle to raise children while seriously sick or to hang onto a job so they'll have money and health insurance. Anyone would be hard pressed to find the energy for spiritual growth when living under such conditions. In so many ways, I remain lucky. Lucky to have survived as well as I have and lucky to be able to tell my story. How I wish I could have acquired what wisdom I might possess without the pain and severe limitations.

Yes, of course MCS radically clipped the wings of my life, but that pruning forced growth in other directions, perhaps as it does for someone who is blinded but finds that his other senses grow stronger as a result. As the outward action of my life diminished, the invisible inside grew stronger. Being housebound was demoralizing, but I became calmer and more centered as a result, the better to tend to my internal life.

Most of what I learned lies beyond words. Such a thing eludes easy explanation. Others saw my life as slow and empty. But inside, a revolution was taking place. Pain and extreme limitations demand depths and dimensions that those easier times don't require. Pain forced me to sort out the strands of my life, to see those spiritual connections all my earlier striving for happiness had not conjured up. My spirituality expanded in quantum leaps. The cloud of unknowing that we all live under opened up on occasions, allowing me so many of those parting sunlit moments of discovery. I often found myself wondering, "Why haven't I noticed this before?" or "Oh, I now get it!" Or I have simply felt the awe of being.

The restrictions of my illness helped me cultivate this contemplative life. My existence wasn't easier, but it was simpler, quieter, less cluttered. There were so many questions to ponder: Why me? What was life all about? How could this new life of mine have meaning? Giving up the idea of controlling my fate helped immensely. But this didn't mean being passive. Rather, it was a balancing act between being purposeful and surrendering myself. Instead of being in the driver's seat, I saw myself as an artist arranging colors handed to me by an unpredictable palette, without knowing what sort of picture would finally emerge.

There was a luminous paradox revealed to me: As my world contracted, in another sense it opened up. I had more internal freedom to explore my beliefs, to find the courage to relinquish what no longer worked or seemed as relevant. Slowly, a whole way of life, a whole new way of understanding, evolved. I understood why Vaclav Havel, president of the Czech and Slovak Federal Republic, thought some of the best years of his life were spent in prison. Or why Nelson Mandela of South Africa once said spending 27 years incarcerated had offered him some advantages. This is a great tragedy, to spend the best years of your life in prison, he admitted, but the experience gave him the chance to think in silence, which is so very hard to do in this outside world. Without prison, he wouldn't have had the opportunity to achieve one of life's most difficult tasks — and that is changing oneself.

Reflection, self-examination, and developing a coherent philosophy of life and ethics require lots of quiet time. Having MCS brought me many of those empty hours waiting to be filled with reflection. Too often I had conducted my life on automatic pilot, not slowing down long enough to contemplate myself or my world. It is so difficult to live in the visible and invisible worlds simultaneously. One tends to pull you away from the other. The active life is compelling but also seductive and deceptive. Changing jobs, remodeling houses, immersing myself in hobbies or sports had kept me busy, but in some ways I remained ignorant of my interior self.

I began to see why some religious people choose a monastic life. Stillness helped strengthen my inner voice. Paring down the active side of life provided clarity. Silence created spaces through which life could find its essential expression, where I could renew myself. We can structure whole lives around achieving and acquiring things of value in the material world. Ultimately, however, I think most of us yearn for spiritual meaning. We want to know the experience of being fully alive, of having purpose to our lives, and to feel that our presence here matters. I began to believe that one of the most central problems of my life was to discover my gifts, and to use them in ways that enrich myself and others. But to find my gifts, I had to discover and strengthen that still-small inner voice.

To survive the experience, to stand up to the skeptics and experts, I had to strengthen my inner voice and convictions. This was one of the ways I had to change myself to create a good life despite those tidal adversities. There was nothing like having my world ripped apart to expose all of my weaknesses. To begin with, I learned that my inner voice needed strengthening after paying a terrible price for listening to the experts and staying in the District building despite my doubts. But trusting my authoritative voice was hard in a society that gives tests, data and experts more credence than human intuition. Now I could also see how much tougher it had been to hear my inner voice when my life overflowed with noise of existence. As a result, I appreciate more than ever the abundance of silence and stillness this illness has brought to my life, even though I would never want to spend another day in bed.

I also learned to stop comparing` my life with other people's or with the dusty, faded photographs of my previous, healthy life. Doing it only caused raw, aching angst because the focus was on what my life lacked. When I compared myself with others, there was always someone doing better than me, even when I was healthy. Of course, when I stacked my life up against another person's, it was never with ill people in Africa who are too poor to afford adequate healthcare or who do not have friends or family to take care of them. No, I would compare myself to healthy people with fortunate lives. When carting my recycle bin full of vitamin bottles out to the curb, the sight of neighbors' bins crammed with wine and soda-pop bottles would leave me jealous. Other people got to drink and take their health for granted, I would think. Other people were able to go on walks without losing brain function. The comparisons could go on and on.

Stopping such patterns of thought helped me to accept the life I had, even if my health never improved. Life could be lived more fully in another measure. I began to welcome the challenge of working on issues like this because the results sent wonderful ripples throughout my life and improved my days immensely. I could see that the quality of my life wasn't affected so much by what happened to me, but instead by what I did with what happened to me. Years after MCS set in, I realized my illness was giving me something like a Ph.D. in the art of living.

Eventually I understood I was becoming healthier in body, mind and soul than I had been before my illness. Surely my body alone was not healthier, but if I considered my whole self – including my mind and soul – I was now in better shape. My definition of health had expanded beyond only my physical body. Maybe I was living differently, but it didn't seem any less valuable. Paradoxically, sometimes at my weakest, I felt my strongest as a whole. I was strong because I could better accept how things really were, because I had to work through my issues more thoroughly. I felt whole because I faced my life head-on, without ignoring or rationalizing the frightening parts or escaping into the distractions of activity.

With time, MCS generated other changes. Having ample time to reflect on the past, I saw what a wonderful life I'd had already. If only I'd recognized this earlier. When people realize this – really know it in their deep heart's core, not just in fleeting moments – it often happens toward the end of life, when the knowledge is good only for the preparations of dying. For me to realize this truth earlier seemed an incredible gift. The tragedy of being sick at an early age had ironically left me with valuable insights when I had so much more real living left to do.

By slowing down, I now saw that my previous hectic life had been like driving down a breathtaking, scenic road at 100 miles per hour. Not only did it limit my experience of life, it had also diminished my capacity to feel and to be thoughtful of others. For instance, I had always known I loved the years my family lived in Egypt. But after my illness, which gave me time for a wider spectrum of emotions, I began to fully realize what an extraordinary experience it had been. My sense of those years then changed from mere fondness to feeling practically heartbroken I will never know that life again. Before, being busy kept me from knowing the full range of my memories and experience. I hadn't adequately digested what those years had meant to me and how the experience had shaped the person I became. My busy life had not only made it more challenging to observe and reflect, but it had also inhibited the development of my wisdom, and my capacity to be my finest self.

One of the most creative responses I could have toward all of the pain and limitation, I concluded, was to be receptive to what it might have to teach me. Indeed, I believed that tragedy could be my finest hour if only I could quarry the crystal from it. I mined a wealth of valuable lessons. For instance, I learned not to analyze other people and their situations. Labeling a person fools us into thinking we understand her or that we're solving her problem. Now, when people share their health troubles with me, as they describe the day-to-day sense of living with a physical mystery, I strive to hear their experience of the situation – not problem-solve by offering a remedy, as if I adequately understand what she's going through. Occasions like these no longer make me nervous about what to say. Illness has taught me that the simple act of listening to a person's experience with an open mind can help lighten her burden.

I have learned again how important it is to have compassion. This quality not only links us to one another, but it cultivates wisdom, leading us to follow certain moral principles. Imagining myself in another person's shoes, the basic act of empathy, even when I don't live with the same circumstances or illness, expands my understanding and leads me to want to treat others with more kindness and respect. It makes me keenly aware of the interdependence of all things. Illness has shown me that compassion can literally help me to become my best self.

Having my body fall apart, and my life along with it, has taught me we have the capacity to start over. Knowing I can survive beginning anew and go on to have a fine life even while under adversity has left me freer to make choices throughout my life. It's helped me see how fear can limit someone in such insidious ways. We pass up so many opportunities because we are afraid of the unknown. As a result, I'm now more relaxed in the presence of uncertainty, although this part is still a work in progress. My faith in life is stronger than it ever has been. MCS has shown me why the very poor and disadvantaged often have more faith than the affluent and fortunate. Faith is something like a muscle. The more you're forced to exercise it because of tough circumstances, the better toned it will be and the more resiliently faithful you tend to become.

One of the toughest lessons involved learning how to create a good day when my body throbbed with pain or when I didn't feel like making the effort. On days when my morning began wearily at 2 a.m., when sickness washed over me like a boiling sea, when overwhelming weakness made the smallest movement tiring, two paths lay before me. The easy route, at least in the short run, would have been to get exasperated, wondering how I was going to get through the day. But this path created a downward spiral, which left me enervated and discouraged. The other route involved acknowledging my feelings, maybe crying out of grief for a few minutes, while disciplining myself to do something that provided pleasure or meaning. So off to the couch I might shuffle to watch a funny movie. Over time, I became more experienced at recognizing these moments that could go either way and disciplined myself to respond constructively. It always took great effort, like how I might have to push myself to exercise at the end of a long day, knowing I would feel better for it in the end.

I learned what it means to be marginalized. One of the most shocking experiences of MCS came from having my status change overnight – from being a valued, respected person to someone others wanted to ignore or get rid of. Being marginalized helped me sympathize with other marginalized people. Now I understand better why, for example, some African-Americans say they prefer out-in-the-open prejudice to hidden racism. For instance, not only was it easier to have my friend Melanie come out and say she found me a hypochondriac, but I also preferred to have doctors openly reject my illness rather than pretend to be scientific to justify their biases. At least I knew what I was dealing with, and others could see the prejudice as well.

Having been exposed to many cultures while living abroad as a child, I came to believe that our culture tends to be a throwaway society, and this has affected my illness experience. Much has been made of the way we often favor throwaway items like plastic shopping bags, disposable diapers, or Styrofoam containers. I think that this throwaway tendency goes much further than that. We sometimes discard relationships as easily, too. We are quick to tear down buildings and replace them with new ones. In the workplace, people are laid off or let go more than in many other countries. Our bias seems to be that newer is preferable, that there will be something better around the corner, and that treating workers as disposable commodities is simply a necessary part of doing business. Out with the old, in with the new. Maybe this is a part of the reason why we seem to love television shows about home improvements and other kinds of makeovers?

I've often wondered how different my illness experience would have been had I been living in another country. Had I not been living in a throwaway society, I might not have fallen ill because my employer might not have constructed a new building but instead made do with the old one; the District might have tried harder to accommodate me and I might not have gotten as sick while trying to do everything I could to hold onto my job; and my marriage might not have been made a casualty. I don't know for sure, but sometimes I wonder.

Society's response to disease is a political issue. I used to understand this only intellectually. Before the onset of MCS, part of me naively believed that new health conditions were evaluated objectively and scientifically, free from bias or other influences. Now I see that with chemical illness, the biggest obstacle is not that we don't know enough about them, or that there isn't enough proof, as the skeptics would have us believe. Rather, the main problem is that powerful businesses, public agencies and individuals don't want to believe it's true. Imagine the mess it will cause if we recognize the harmful effects of common, everyday chemicals. Virtually all employers would have to change the way they do business, government would have to come up with new regulations, medical schools would have to train doctors about a new health condition, insurance companies would have to cover a new illness, and so on. No wonder resistance is so fierce.

Think of how many decades it took for us to acknowledge the potentially harmful effects of cigarette smoking – decades during which research studies and evidence piled up while the tobacco industry tried to stifle the emerging information. And that was only a single harmful substance, which was far easier to prove than the complex effects of the hundreds of chemicals each us can be exposed to simply by breathing.

I've learned there is a difference between intellect and wisdom. For me, intellect involves my ability to learn or reason or think abstractly, whereas wisdom is a knowing that comes from listening to myself and paying attention to the rhythms of inner experience. Since becoming ill, I've developed the belief that we don't appreciate and honor being wise nearly enough. I've been struck by how my upbringing provided me with a fine intellectual education and exposed me to various cultures, but no one helped me to develop my wisdom, which I think is probably typical for most children. Yet it is wisdom that has carried me through my illness and has contributed most to my happiness. For me, one of the great things about cultivating ways to become wise is that whatever happens to me in life – the good moments, hard times, and occasional failures – all of it can contribute toward my wisdom if I can digest and learn from the experience.

When dealing with some doctors and air quality experts over the course of my illness, I've often wished they had more wisdom. Sometimes so much emphasis gets placed upon developing one's intellect when training for a profession, the cultivation of wisdom lags behind. I couldn't expect those experts to be wise about my own particular sickness. To be so, they would have had to have personal experience with it. But I believe it might have helped if they could have been wise about knowing themselves to begin with. Perhaps if they could have been more conscious of their biases and any anxiety they might feel when faced with the limits of their knowledge, then maybe they wouldn't have resorted to psychological explanations for my sickness so quickly. The best doctors were the ones who seemed to have wisdom, who could listen to and respect my experiences with my body, then put it together with their knowledge to come up with advice or a plan.

In time I realized it wasn't enough to have profound experiences that woke me up or to learn lessons through pain and limitation. I had to grow into those experiences, to develop myself more completely, so the insights and changes could take root and blossom into full life. My newfound knowledge needed time and ongoing work to penetrate into my deepest self. In an unexpected way, that's where having my illness drag on for years came in handy. The sickness kept my feet to that spiritual fire and provided the ongoing motivation to make sure I was following through with all I had learned.

As the years passed after I fell ill, I found I had less of a sense of permanent self. My experiences, personality and skills did not seem to belong specifically to me. While moving through the day, I felt as if life were a song being sung through me. The boundary between myself and the world had softened. As a result, I felt deeply connected to everything around me. It was an indescribable experience of being deeply at one with life.

Daily meditation fostered this personal growth. It turned out the most useful form of meditation involved observing my body, even the painful parts. Certainly dwelling too much on my troubles could make them worse, but that didn't mean disregarding them was any better. I found that escape didn't help in the long run. The ignoring strategy had often been my way of coping with intermittent arthritis pain for years. But this illness taught me that in tuning out something as powerful as physical suffering, other parts of me got shut down as well. I could not repress selectively. For me, learning to remain aware of all aspects of my life led to more clarity and energy. It helped me solve problems and apply myself more creatively.

Meditation also helped me live more in the moment – a useful result, since the moment is all we have. When I lived mindfully, when I could view life immediately without ignoring the unpleasant parts, I felt the most fully alive. Rather than rushing through the dishes to sit down and read the newspaper, I stayed aware of what my hands were doing; instead of resenting the time it took to prepare meals while flinging food into pots, my focus shifted to how food nourished me and how I enjoyed the act of creating. Not doing several things at once made me more content and less harried, if not as productive. It helped me be my best self. I appreciated the days more. Life had more dimension to it, and the smallest details could have a sense of wonder. Gradually, partly because of my illness experience as well as meditation, the ordinary could feel extraordinary.

The best advice I heard to reduce stress – allow twice as much time for an activity as you think you'll need – enhanced living in the present moment. For me, the suggestion was more effective than the more common adage "Try to do less." The effort improved the quality of my days. It also came to alter and enhance my perceptions. I saw the glories of the day under a new light.

One winter morning, I woke to a fairyland of cotton-candy snow, an uncommon sight in Seattle. In the old days, I would have spent the morning caught up in the details of getting to work, sliding down steep, icy hills to reach the District. Instead, that morning the world seemed magical. I reveled in its jewel-like splendor. Somehow the snow seemed more beautiful than ever before, like glittering diamonds encrusting the houses and gardens. I breathed in the hush of the streets more now than in the past, in the suspension of airplane and car traffic, at times punctuated by the shrieks of delighted children sliding down our hilly street. Everything seemed to be in concert.

Eventually I realized, too, that my particular sickness was far more effective training for living in the moment than meditation. When I feel pain in my leg or notice the early signs of an upset stomach, the symptoms draw me into the present and force me to pay attention to everything to keep the situation from deteriorating. Pain forces this kind of contracted attention span. To minimize my health troubles, I periodically check in with myself during the day to see if there is anything I need to do, any adjustment I need to make, to keep from getting sicker, and in an unexpected way the effort ends up reinforcing living in the moment. But most of all, the sickness trains me for living in the present because with my illness, this moment is all I can be sure of. When I was healthy, I used to live as if I had forever ahead of me. Now I don't put things off into some distance. Nevertheless, I don't strive to live in the moment every minute of the day because sometimes it's necessary to reflect upon the past or to spend time planning for the future.

These years have been punctuated by moments of the most intense joy. I thought I had known joy before, but this was something else again. It was a rich, voluptuous joy. After I became ill, the mere sight of cherry trees in bloom took my breath away. Eating lunch outside on my porch on sunny winter days wasn't just pleasant, it felt sublime. Intense pain had created a sense of gratitude in me on a scale I hadn't had when healthy, and it led to this deeper joy.

Everyone will have a different definition of joy. For me it's a state of pleasure or happiness, which bubbles up from a deep place and endures longer than things or moments that bring those more transitory pleasures, like eating a piece of chocolate cake. Joy is more of a sustained state, although not a constant one. When healthy, I wouldn't have made much distinction between the two because I didn't give the topic much thought. Life was pleasant enough that I didn't need to. And too often, my feelings of happiness were dependent upon achieving something or a participating in a longed-for event, such as a new job or a trip. Then once I'd gotten what I wanted, I would adapt to what I had desired or achieved within a few months and would start yearning for something else to get me back to feeling high levels of happiness again. Life was going by so quickly that I didn't even know I was missing out on feeling a sustained state of joy.

If you had asked me back then if I experienced much joy, I would have said yes but that's because I hadn't tasted much of it and didn't know the difference. If my illness hadn't narrowed my life so severely, I might not have known the experience and thus discovered the value and power of joy. These days I pay closer attention to what actually brings me joy. Appreciating life's more fleeting pleasures is still important to me, and I make a place for them as well, but that more deeply interfused joy is now my priority.

I now have a different relationship to sadness and pain. Formerly, I used to want to know happiness but avoid sadness and pain as much as possible. I thought dodging pain would translate into more happiness. But I've realized it's hard for me to experience the highest peaks of joy if I haven't known deep valleys of sadness and pain. They're emotions along the same spectrum, a sort of package deal. Suppressing sadness at one end of the range seems to diminish joy at the other end. It is similar to how if you close your heart to hurt, you often shut yourself off from love and other emotions. For me, knowing more intense pain has stimulated a more exquisite joy, the most profound paradox of my illness experience. It's like how after suffering from a virulent flu, just being able to stand up and walk around or to eat tends to feel so much more wonderful than it does on an ordinary day when your body is working well enough.

I don't mean I welcome pain and sadness or I wallow in it, because part of me wants to avoid it. I just no longer fight or repress the experience itself. I allow myself to know it and then to move beyond it. This has added the benefit of feeling a broader range and intensity of emotions, which seems to have also opened me up to more depth of experience.

Sometimes, in the past, I anesthetized myself with things like food or shopping or hobbies to avoid pain or sadness. Unfortunately, doing so seemed to inadvertently sedate my nerve endings for joy. But when this major illness came along and involved such intense, long-lasting suffering that I couldn't avoid it with the usual escapes, I had to admit the pain. While some have told me I've allowed myself to get too upset over my sickness, I'd like to say to them that I now believe people who feel the full depths of their pain or who allow themselves to fully grieve in response to life's problems may be closer to something like "mental health" than those who do not. People who appear even-tempered and calm in the face of serious pain or catastrophe can have a grim, stoic quality about them, perhaps because of all the suffering that has been suppressed along the way as they've tried to be happy.

The day we at the District moved to the new building, I had no idea those moorings of my old life had been forever severed. I was busy making sure my work files and supplies had arrived intact in my new office, unaware that my world was about to be torn asunder. But then I didn't realize I was on the verge of embarking on a journey to that vast undiscovered country within. Who would have guessed the impending trip would be just as exotic, perhaps even more so, as my most far-flung travels? Or that the journey would leave me with a rich legacy the world could not take away?

My odyssey has come at a high price. I am not glad to have spent so much time and money on my health, in the prime of my life, or to be unable to work and travel. Nor have I enjoyed the isolation and limited diet. I wish the experience hadn't been so hard on everyone around me, or that it hadn't involved many losses. No, it hasn't been a journey I would sign up for. But, oh, what a remarkable adventure it has been.

Afterword

In the end, since my illness is a chronic one with no known cure, I've found it more powerful to strive to transcend it rather than to hope it will miraculously go away or that it will be solved by more health therapies. Sometimes, making the effort to do this takes all the courage and energy I can muster. It's difficult, but in the long run, finding ways to transcend the illness helps me avoid getting mired in my limitations.

⁓

By the time I arrived at the Air France gate at Seattle-Tacoma International Airport on a soggy July afternoon, the place throbbed with summer travelers standing in lines that stretched like long pearl necklaces as far as the eye could see. The day had started out like any other trip to France, but somehow everything was different. I felt like Cinderella who had gotten to go to the ball after all, although if you had seen me with my face mask on, being pushed along in a wheelchair, a lumbar roll pillow behind my back, the word Cinderella might not be the word that would come to mind. Nevertheless, every detail thrilled me: flight attendants welcoming us on board, passengers putting their luggage into overhead compartments, announcements in French.

Looking around, part of me felt incredulous that everyone went about their business so casually, as if this was nothing special. How was this so? I wondered. I wanted to shout, "Don't you realize how lucky you are? You can cross an ocean without your health disintegrating! You can move your bodies as you see fit!" Feelings of intense gratitude would continue to wash over me throughout the trip.

Once in Paris, I walked over to my friend Jacques' apartment on a warm velvet night, on one of the few days when it hadn't rained on my vacation in Paris. As I wandered along the Seine River, passing by the stately Assemblée Nationale building with the Grand Palais in the distance, the sight nearly overwhelmed me. I felt so filled up with beauty, so drunk with pleasure. Many times in years past, I had walked along this river, down the same street, past the same buildings, and found them exquisite. But they had never looked as impossibly ravishing as they did this time. After years of being housebound by illness, the sights dazzled me. They almost blinded me.

Jacques and I drank champagne in his apartment, looking out at the ornate gold wedding-cake dome under which Napoleon is buried, and at the Eiffel Tower, as we caught up on each other's lives. Afterward, we strolled across the esplanade to a restaurant for what would be one of the most memorable dinners I'd had in 15 years, and certainly the biggest. Jacques ordered for the two of us, and the plates began to flow like a rhapsody from the kitchen. Thick slices of silky foie gras. Escargots nestled on triangular pieces of toast, set on a bed of rock salt, brought with small silver clamps and forks to pull the snails out of their shells.

I mentioned to Jacques that I was a little embarrassed to have to ask him not to wear cologne since he works for a large fragrance company. Surprisingly, though, it's easier for me to tolerate fragrances here in Paris, where the French even perfume some of their buses and subways.

"Americans," Jacques said, "tend to like their products as cheap as possible. So we manufacture different fragrances for the U.S. market, and some of the ingredients we use are illegal in other countries." Behind him, the doors had been flung open to the balmy night air, and the light shining on Napoleon's gold dome threw its spire of rich ornamentation into sharp relief. "The French would be suspicious of such ingredients."

I was intrigued by this information. In France, I'd enjoyed significantly better health, which had made me curious. I'd taken other fun and exciting holidays in the United States since my illness, but I didn't experience such significant health improvements in those places.

Memories surfaced about something one of my alternative healthcare providers said to me before I departed for Paris. She told me, "I think you'll be able to eat as much cheese as you want over there, as long as you buy fresh, regional cheese because the exported ones have preservatives in them. The French have much cleaner cheese than we do." Still, I had been skeptical of her prediction because for 14 years I hadn't been able to eat cheese without dire health effects, except for tiny amounts every now and then. But lo and behold, she was right. As a result, I had been feasting on various cheeses each day. Sometimes I'd even eat them at breakfast. I'd also found that cheese and many other foods in Paris spoil about three times faster than my food at home.

It turns out the French have not only minimized their exposure to chemicals in food more than Americans have, but they have minimized the exposure in their air — at least with the pollutants I'm sensitive to — and their office buildings as well. French laws require three times as much ventilation as American standards do, and French buildings generally consume only half the energy of American buildings. In Europe, the windows in most skyscrapers open because air-conditioning is controlled room by room, whereas in the United States windows are usually sealed shut and office buildings depend on central air-conditioning. Most European building codes also require all workers to have access to a window. In addition, Europeans use powerful air filters and tend to circulate the air three times as frequently as in America.

Construction in Europe does cost more — an average of 50 percent more per square foot. But American researchers have estimated U.S. companies could save as much as $200 billion annually in worker performance improvements and $58 billion by preventing sick-building illnesses. At the very least, artificial air can contribute toward making desk workers in office buildings more lethargic and sleepy.

I thought again about my sense of how the French tend to value quality over quantity and how they're willing to pay more for it. Memories of my perfume-wearing days before my sickness came to mind, of how I would choose several modestly priced different fragrances to have a variety — without questioning what ingredients were in them and what their possible health effects were — instead of paying more for a single perfume that didn't stress my liver or immune system. When making purchases, I often emphasized getting a lot for my money without much regard for long-term consequences, such as for my health or the environment. I think about the American expressions that reveal the value we place on money, such as "Time is money" and "You look like a million dollars." In many other countries, people wouldn't know what you mean; if you told them that they look like money, it might be taken as an insult rather than a compliment.

Even when I think about the idea of the American dream, much of it involves quantity over quality; for instance, owning a large home and making a good salary. The French tend to define themselves differently. It's not, I believe, that they are against having large homes or lots of money so much as that they have other priorities including family, relationships, love, community, celebration and good taste. Since falling ill, I've felt too much value gets placed on things that can be quantified in the United States, like how many boards you sit on or how many interesting trips you've taken or how much money you make – instead of focusing on things that represent quality, such as being a kind, loving person or facing life's challenges with grace.

Another factor may have influenced the health improvements I experienced in France. One of the people on my healthcare team, who has the best track record at understanding my body's seeming whims and who predicted I'd be able to eat cheese over there, believes my body was working harder in Paris because it was in a completely different environment. Changing the pattern puts the body into a survival state, she explained, which makes your organ systems run more efficiently. It's the same reason two men can lift an automobile during a fire when normally they're not capable of it. Her thoughts made me think about how I do something like this with my stomach medications. When I take one drug for my digestive problems every day, I find that after one month it's no longer doing much for me. But if I have four different medications and rotate them every two weeks, they continue to work.

It's not as if I didn't have health problems in France, but they were less severe. There, I felt as if I had the flu most of the time, whereas in Seattle my illness can seem more like food poisoning. In Paris, I actually had occasional days when I felt well, which hardly ever happens in Seattle. As a result, I could carry on more easily in France, even when not feeling well, and have moments that felt almost like those of a normal life. But I also had additional problems in France, such as my feet often burned with pain and swelling and my legs with muscle spasms.

Toward the end of my holiday in France, after returning from a train trip to visit the Dondeys at their home in the Alps, pigeon-clucking noises rose in my stomach before I even left the train station. My brain felt as if it was shivering. By the next day, my last day in France, I was so nauseated, I didn't know whether I'd be able to get on an airplane the following day. Despair engulfed me. Couldn't I have a two-and-a-half-week break from this business? Was it too much to ask? My thoughts turned to how difficult it might be to reschedule a flight during the height of tourist season and of how much money it would cost.

જ

As I reflect upon it now, one of the biggest surprises of my sickness is that I am able to live beyond the boundaries of my limitations. I am surprised by the joy that I am more because of this experience, even though my body is less and my life has seen major losses. The severity of my initial limitations have expanded me in many ways, and they continue to enlarge me, a paradox I am only now beginning to understand 16 years after falling ill. Through these limitations, I now realize, I've become someone I wouldn't have been had I remained healthy.

Even my mind has expanded because I now use more of its capacity. For years I grieved over the cognitive losses caused by my sickness – my poor memory and slower word-finding ability, for example – but I overlooked something important. Before the sickness, I had primarily used the left side of my brain because my education and upbringing had trained me in that direction. But when faced with a mysterious illness of staggering proportions, the logical and linear part of my mind was woefully inadequate for the challenge. I had to think outside of the normal channels, to be more open-minded and exploratory. And so without realizing it, out of necessity, I developed the right side of my brain as well. But like my illness, the change might not show up on standard cognitive tests. Becoming more creative, imaginative and flexible, I think, has been essential in transcending tragedy.

I used to think of creativity in a literal way, such as when an artist paints or composes music. But now I see that creative skills can be used in aspects of living, in how we give shape to our lives. In that sense, even a scientist or physician can be creative if he takes his knowledge and puts it together in a new way. Between the way I'm now living through both sides of my brain and in a concert of body, mind *and* soul, I feel I

181

have more capacity and that I'm drawing upon more of my potential. This has transformed my world from black-and-white monochrome to vibrating colors. It has provided me a scope for living that I never could have dreamed would be possible.

At times, having to measure and assess and calculate what my health can handle makes me feel weary and exasperated. But those efforts have spilled over into other areas of my life and have left significant benefits in their wake. Noticing how exposures to chemicals affect my health motivates me to think everything through more deeply and thoroughly before I act. In my healthy days, I did not do this enough. For instance, I would often get enthusiastic about an opportunity of some sort or agree to something because it was expected of me, and end up taking on too much. Then, even though the opportunity was something I should enjoy, being too busy or preoccupied drained some of the fun out of it or I would end up spending too much time on things that weren't important to me. I would chide myself for over-committing, but much of the time it came from not paying adequate attention in the first place and not being realistic enough.

My illness stimulated me to develop the skill for assessing my life on this day or in this moment well enough that it has become another habit of being, which leads to a more enjoyable existence. As a result, I have far fewer regrets and more ability to create the life I want. More importantly, the unrelenting nature of the sickness keeps me from forgetting to use the skill because there may be hell to pay if I make the wrong judgment call. The price of landing in bed feeling poisoned, because I have taken on too much, is just too high.

Although my life still teems with many restrictions, I now have a different relationship to them. I've discovered that sometimes less is more, that having a lot of choices and opportunities doesn't always lead to more happiness and can eat up a lot of time. As much as possible, I now choose quality over quantity. When healthy, I made many assumptions about what would make for a happier, better-quality life and often didn't notice when they didn't turn out to be true. Then severe physical limitations made me observe everything more closely because, in a way, my life depended upon it.

Ultimately what I've discovered is that much of the time it's not getting everything I want that brings me joy so much as appreciating what I already have. And a surprising variation on my less-is-more discovery involves how I've found that sometimes too much of a good thing can actually dull my senses and my level of appreciation or pleasure for it. I do feel disappointed when I have to cancel plans to go to a friend's house for a holiday dinner, for instance, but I no long rail against a lost opportunity because I know the next holiday when I get to go will be all the sweeter, that I will revel in every detail more intensely. It's perhaps like how much more special strawberry shortcake tastes because the fruit is in season for only a few weeks each year.

Today my health is improved, but I'm nowhere near being able to hold down a job. I am back to eating 80 percent of all foods, which, considering how much I love food and cooking, has brought back a nearly daily joy to my life. My weight is finally normal. When getting together with other people these days, I have to ask them only not to wear perfume, cologne and hairspray rather than to shower first with my unscented soap and shampoo. These days I wear a mask only 10 percent to 30 percent of the time when going out, depending on how my sensitivities are that day.

Yet my health still ebbs and flows. The causes can't always be discerned. At one point, my tolerance for food and chemicals improved dramatically, but the change lasted only eight months. This past year, I was in a downward spiral for 10 months, the worst I have known in eight years. After six months of it, my symptoms had worsened so much that I couldn't leave the house without wearing a mask and my digestion was upset daily, confining me to bed much of the time. When friends would call me to propose meeting for lunch, I would have to say, "I'm under house arrest!" They often came to my house instead.

I knew I had to try to find new health therapies because the existing ones weren't doing enough. At first the thought of having to run around to new health practitioners, to tell my unusual health history to one more person, to be patient while that person went through the usual steep learning curve to figure out whether he or she could help me, felt exasperating and exhausting. But the effort paid off.

I was referred to a Chinese doctor who practices traditional Chinese medicine and who works on many different levels – through acupuncture, Chinese herbal teas and pills, a breathing meditation, Chi Gong and Tai Chi, to name a few – and the results of her work have been surprisingly powerful. All of the different therapies were designed to address my particular energetic weaknesses and imbalances. I think such a seamless integration of treatments, all designed toward the same goal, has had a synergistic effect, which has been greater than each treatment would have been on its own. My Chinese doctor is the first person I've found in 15 years who has been able to help me with some of my more severe problems. It sometimes feels like a small miracle. Her work has improved six of my health problems so significantly that my days in bed have been reduced by nearly 70 percent.

I find it sobering that if it weren't for this doctor and another alternative healthcare provider, at this point I would be an invalid. Both alternative providers and an osteopath now comprise the mainstay of my health treatments, together with mainstream physicians who treat me for various health symptoms. The osteopath keeps my body in alignment, which has helped my overall health.

As for the health of others who were sickened by the District building 16 years ago, I am still in touch with only three of them. I am not in contact with anyone working in the building today. Joan Bell was laid off years ago, and although she had planned to work for another five years, she was not terribly disappointed because she was eligible for retirement. Today Joan is in fine health, although occasionally she gets sickened by very powerful smells.

Helen Smith, in the Equal Employment Opportunity Department, found that her building-related health problems developed into two forms of arthritis. In the beginning, when her doctors kept diagnosing her with various illnesses, they gave her large doses of Prednisone, which caused diabetes. They told Helen it would go away once she was off the medication, but that did not happen. Today Helen cannot work. She receives a small monthly Social Security disability check. Even though Helen hired my lawyer for her workers' compensation case, she did not win.

Marketing manager David Hall's shortness of breath went away after one year in the new building, so he thought the office was no longer affecting his health. But another health problem appeared. David developed sciatica pain, which his doctors attributed to general wear and tear. Eventually he was referred to a neurologist who diagnosed him with Parkinson's disease. Seven years after moving into the building, David Hall was forced to take an early retirement after 20 years with the District. His wife had to take early retirement as well to take care of him. He does not receive any workers' compensation. Before leaving, David applied for the District's private disability insurance, from which he receives $54 a month. I think about their losses, their lives now, and how my own story relates.

Ted and I are now divorced, but I have chosen not to tell that part of the story.

❧

So much of my life has been swept out to sea by this sickness: my marriage, my ability to work, my chance to have children, my capacity to go here and there without scrupulous planning. Grief and loss have become a thread inextricably woven throughout the fabric of my life. Somehow, though, I've learned how to create a good life despite it all, and that has been my salvation.

After all of the losses and crises, I know the value of having good health, of being able to count on my body to do the simple things of living. The first eight years of my illness were the hardest, so densely laden were they with losses and crises, some of them too painful to recount, that for me, just to spend a quiet evening at home without such drama as background noise can feel almost glorious. One day I was talking with my therapist, Sally Newell, about how much more I was appreciating my life because of I what I was going through. She said to me: "I'm going to tell you a little secret. People who have experienced extraordinary suffering and who have found a way to transcend it are usually happier than regular-happy people." Indeed this has proved to be true for me.

❧

Ironically, growing up the way I did put me at a disadvantage once illness struck, because all of my family's travels and numerous activities made it harder for me to appreciate a simple life and how wonderful it can be. Since my illness, I've sometimes thought about how some children today grow up with schedules jam-packed with activities like sports practices, music lessons and play dates, and I wonder if they're going to have the same trouble I did being happy leading a simple life and appreciating life's small pleasures. I'm not against activities, but now I value finding a balance between doing and being. I have had to work on this balance in order to create a quality life. My ability to appreciate my simplified life was made even more difficult by an unspoken message of my upbringing and Princeton education: that if I wasn't doing something big and grand with my life, then it didn't amount to much. Thankfully, today I can feel content just being – letting the day soak in, sitting in my garden listening to the birds sing, reading a good book, enjoying the company of friends.

Surprisingly, I have found unexpected pleasure in discovering that other people value me simply for who I am rather than for what I do, or for other surface trappings of my life. I had never thought about this before my sickness, but our friendships and relationships are often based upon feeling common ground with someone because you share similar careers or hobbies, or you have children who are good friends, and that is a fine basis for relationship. Sometimes people are even drawn to someone else because they're fascinated by that person's line of work or lifestyle. But illness stripped away the veneer of my outer life dramatically. I have no job, no husband, no children. For 16 years, I have lived largely housebound. My poor health has made it difficult to pursue some of my passions and hobbies or to take on certain types of volunteer work. Yet my friends have wanted to continue walking alongside me, which is also a testament to the quality of people they are. Despite the severe limitations of my life, I have still made new friends. Knowing that others value me simply for who I am, even with this stripped-down life, rather than for what I do or for a long list of accomplishments, has been profoundly satisfying.

Another important gift is the close relationship I now have with my soul. Somehow, as the blazing fire of my sickness motivated me to find additional internal resources to cope, I stumbled onto a greater, more powerful place within myself, which I call my soul. Each person will have a different definition and experience of this, for in a way we're all like blind men touching various parts of an elephant – some feel his trunk, others his tail or foot. This results in each of us having different perspectives on what an elephant is. For me, the soul seems to abide in its mystery, but these days it's more of a partner, instead of a shadowy presence, and the difference has been profound. It means I have a greater capacity to be my finest self and to achieve my dreams. Strength and love now flow more abundantly in my life, both in giving and in receiving love. When I tapped into my soul, I connected to a powerful love deep within that I already possessed but had not accessed before. So now, instead of seeking love through relationships with others, I simply *am* love, which enables me to enjoy relationships all the more. I feel as if I used to be a fish in an ocean when I was healthy, only dimly aware of the other world and life that was taking place on land. My close partnership with my soul has exposed me to a world I could never have imagined existed before and has made so much more possible.

This change doesn't mean I get everything I want, because being in perfect health would be at the top of my list, of course. But it does mean I'm now less dependent on my life turning out a particular way to know deep joy. As a result of this transformation, I've had significantly more success with changing myself and creating the life I desire. I now agree with Nelson Mandela that changing oneself is one of life's most difficult tasks. For me, it's been crucial for transcending a major illness and finding ways to have a good life despite it.

Although I feel as if I've earned a Ph.D. in the art of living, I strive for balance and moderation, even within my unexpected spiritual journey. I know I'm influenced by my culture, which tends to be forever driven toward achievement – whether it's in the form of exploring experiences like personal and spiritual growth or getting our bodies into athletic shape – and that an unrelenting drive to better myself can diminish the quality of my life rather than enhance it. The intense emphasis on self-improvement in the United States can, for instance, leave me with the feeling that nothing is ever good enough and that there is always something more I could be doing to enrich my life. Too much achievement can do the opposite of what I seek and make me feel lonelier, more preoccupied and stressed, and unsure of who I am. In the United States, we excel at working very hard, I believe – not just at our jobs, but in our personal lives as well – and the trait certainly has benefits, for example, by contributing toward a sound economy. However, we're not great at the art of living. Thus, I believe in moderation – even moderation *in moderation!* Still, my illness has taught me that cultivating a close relationship with my soul is definitely a self-improvement effort worth making. It's just that now I pay attention to whether I'm sometimes pushing myself too hard. Because I ask myself, what good is such a self-improvement or spiritual journey effort if it leads to diminished joy?

Today, if I were asked what I think is one of the most important qualities to have when facing such a sickness, I'd have to say it would be tenacity – the ability to keep on keeping on, even when I feel like giving up, even when the situation looks hopeless, even when I don't think I have enough strength to carry on. Perseverance requires courage, though, because I have to carry on despite feelings of fear and despair; and because at the end of the day, I don't know which efforts will bear fruit. But I believe that even if I can't be cured of my illness, tenacity has helped me find ways to bring a measure of meaning and quality of life into my days, and to find opportunities within my misfortune.

To me, the other most important quality to have when facing a major mysterious illness is the ability to take personal responsibility for coping with it. Since I have a sickness that isn't yet in the medical books, and because there are no proven treatments for it, the burden has fallen on me to learn all I can about it and come up with ways to deal with and hopefully improve it. If I hadn't done this, I might have lapsed into seeing myself as a victim and ended up a bitter, angry person. In a way, letting myself become a victim would have been the easier route, the path of least resistance.

In the very beginning of my sickness, I certainly felt angry toward the doctors and other experts who suspected they had a hypochondriac on their hands, and at the District staff who I felt distanced themselves from me, and at the few who practically treated me as a whistleblower for suggesting that our beautiful new office building might be making some people sick. Questions like, "Why did this happen to me?" surged through my mind. But in hindsight, I can see that at some point I realized I had a choice between taking responsibility for myself and my health or being passive in the face of it, and I decided upon the former path. At the time, it felt as if I was groping and stumbling around in the dark, but a part of me could see what a depressing existence I might have if I didn't make a major effort to manage it. I knew I didn't want to squander my life.

If faced with the same situation again, because of my illness experience, I would handle it more consciously. I would ask myself, "Who do I want to be? An angry and bitter person beaten down by misfortune, or someone who finds a way to transcend her illness?" And if I chose to try to rise above the sickness, I would ponder ways to go about becoming the person I wanted to be. Today I often ask myself this question, even when facing situations that don't involve my health. Who do I want to be, even when no one's watching me or even when I'm not getting credit for it? Illness has taught me that who I am affects not only everything I do, but also my experience of life. Once I ask myself the question, my priorities and the actions I need to take become much clearer.

∾

Shortly after returning to Seattle from France, I began to dream of living in Paris for three or four months each year. Because my health had fared so much better in France, my holiday there was the closest I'd had to a normal life in 14 years. Mainly, I wanted to live in Paris so I could spend part of the year tasting a normal life and picking up where I left off with my French friends. I hoped I also might experience other health benefits there. For instance, I put on muscle during my two-week vacation because I could walk and move about more freely. As a result, my chronic neck pain and dizziness disappeared. At home, I can't exercise much without triggering pain or injury.

I also longed to rediscover my adventurous, travel-loving nature, which had lain dormant for far too long. After having grown up abroad, I yearned to spend part of each year in another society that offers those traits I have missed in the United States. The way the French place more

189

value on relationships, community, wisdom, and pleasure of life and of the senses resonates with me. And being in a city so steeped in beauty could inspire me. There are many things I enjoy about the United States as well, but for me, no one culture has it all. I find American society to be young and brash, partly because we are such a new country, and France has more age and experience, though there is much to savor about both. Most of all, I dreamed of spending part of the year in Paris because with an ongoing serious illness, I have to find ways to make my life fresh, to replenish myself in ways both small and large. Otherwise, the unrelenting daily grind of it all could wear me down to a pulp.

The challenge is keeping my life from becoming a vacuum, isolated and sealed off from the outside world. And most days a layer of my stamina and time automatically gets siphoned off to managing the sickness, or on some days just surviving it. Being sick every day of my life can be a profoundly depressing experience. It's the same thing time after time, one symptom or another crying out for attention, although the severity of them vacillates. The whole business can have a deadening effect on my spirit. To counteract this bleeding effect, I have to find ways to bring fresh blood into my life whether in the form of new experiences or ideas or relationships. So I ask myself what inspires me or stimulates me or causes me to see things in a different manner. It takes imagination and effort because I can't simply pluck ideas out of the air, like apples from a tree. For years I have made life new and different in small ways like taking a class or planning a garden. Now that I get to have dreams again, I hope to live in Paris.

My Paris dream also came up because illness and disability have caused me to change my priorities. As I've reflected upon how I haven't been able to have a career or children and so many other experiences, I've realized there were still things in life I desired that might yet be possible. Having a magnificent moment in my life then became a priority, which is why I've been willing to spend huge amounts of effort and money to go to Paris.

Right now I'm so glad I'm single because I love the idea of being able to go back and forth between Seattle and Paris. Life continues to surprise me. Not only am I amazed I'm able to pick up and live in Paris, but I would not have expected I'd enjoy being single as much as I have. While the first year after getting divorced was filled with anguish and heart-wrenching loneliness, grieving over all of my losses, once I adjusted I found I was having a fine time. I loved being married, except for the very last years, but I also love being single. For me, each state has its own characteristics, and there is much to enjoy on both sides of the fence. I have found that being single provides a much better chance to develop my interior self, so I have tried to take advantage of the opportunity. Some of my greatest inspiration, insights and creativity have come to me in solitude. In that sense, my recent life has been a rich and precious time.

So as I sit and write, I am reminded that in a few weeks I leave for Paris to try out living there for three or four months. Setting off on such a venture reminds me I'm well beyond survival living, at least for the moment, and that I still get to have dreams and follow them. It has taken one year of additional health treatments and meticulous planning with several healthcare providers to make this undertaking possible. All of the effort required for a mere three to four months away has sometimes felt staggering and exhausting. Seemingly simple things have teemed with complications, such as securing housing that doesn't aggravate my health. Paris has had a housing shortage for years, so the supply of furnished rentals is limited. My health requirements then reduce the small pool by about 90 percent. I need an apartment building with an elevator, which cuts out about half of all rentals. I can't stay in a place that's had animals, and so on. Most rental agencies will not show clients their apartments, and it's risky for me to take a place if I haven't been able to walk around it and smell it, to lie down and try out the bed. Exchanging my home with that of someone in Paris won't work because of the odors and fragrances people would bring into my house. I still don't know where I'm going to live in Paris. Finding housing is only one piece of the puzzle I face.

Sometimes I doubt I'll be able to pull off this adventure. In other moments I'm frightened, the more so because I'm going alone and I really won't know until I've been there for a while whether I'll be well enough to enjoy myself. During last summer's trip to France, my sickness certainly made the undertaking harder and more stressful. It's difficult enough to be sick at home but harder still in an unfamiliar setting, in a country where I'm not fluent in the language, don't fully understand the nuances of the culture, and don't know where to buy necessary products. Only time will tell whether all of the effort I've had to expend, and will continue to have to make once in Paris, will have seemed worth it. Why am I doing this? I sometimes ask myself. What made me think I could go? Now that the trip draws near and the complications are multiplying, every single day I must consciously choose to make this a joyful and positive experience, and to remind myself the adventure is possible. Once in Paris, I will need to discipline myself to continue doing this because, between feeling sick much of the time and with all I'll have to do to pull everything off, feeling joyful and positive about being in Paris won't happen automatically, as it did when I was healthy. Making my dream possible is turning out to require huge courage, focus and intention.

Sometimes the thought of going there makes me laugh uncontrollably. In my healthy years, Ted and I stopped in Paris every year or two to see his sister and her family, and back then as we wandered about the city I thought I knew roughly how my life would play out – that I'd be working and unable to do something like living in France, that moving to a new office building would be exciting, that I'd be married to Ted for the rest of my life, that we would eventually have children. How wrong I was about every part of it. Nothing has gone according to plan. But a side of me finds it funny because in certain respects, I never could have foreseen an adventure as amazing as the one I'm on.

Sometimes I think about the adage "When one door closes, another one opens" and how even though the world was shut off from me for so long, after about 13 years some doors did begin to open and it just keeps getting better. I still wish I enjoyed good health. But now, as I look to be able to live in Paris for part of the year, to have my body, mind and soul indulge in its sensuous, moveable feast, I feel renewed and hopeful like a verdant spring. I can't believe how well my life has turned out.

Selected Readings

Chemical Exposures: Low Levels and High Stakes (1998) by Nicholas A. Ashford and Claudia S. Miller; John Wiley & Sons.

Nontoxic, Natural & Earthwise: How to Protect Yourself and Your Family From Harmful Products and Live in Harmony with the Earth (1990) by Debra Lynn Dadd, Judy Collins and Steve Lett; Penguin Group.

At the Will of the Body: Reflections on Illness (1991) by Arthur W. Frank; Houghton Mifflin.

Meet Your Soul. Stretch Your Wings and Fly: Connecting with Your Quantum Power (2007) by Maxine Jones; Cherry Tree Publishing.

Full Catastrophe Living: Using the Wisdom of Your Body and Mind to Face Stress, Pain, and Illness (1990) by Jon Kabat-Zinn, Ph.D.; Dell Publishing.

Living with Multiple Chemical Sensitivity: Narratives of Coping (2000), Gail McCormick; McFarland & Company.

Medicine and Culture: Varieties of Treatment in the United States, England, West Germany, and France (1996) by Lynn Payer; Henry Holt and Company.

Diet for a Poisoned Planet: How to Choose Safe Foods for You and Your Family: The Twenty-first Century Edition (2006) by David Steinman; Perseus Publishing.

The Pendulum and the Toxic Cloud: The Course of Dioxin Contamination (1979) by Thomas Whiteside; Yale University Press.

About the Author

Anne Lipscomb is a former award-winning public relations manager who developed multiple chemical sensitivity in 1993. She became one of a handful of people in Washington state to receive workers' compensation for illness related to sick-building syndrome. Born in Texas, Anne spent most of her childhood in Africa and traveling in other parts of the world with her parents and lived as an exchange student in India and France. Anne has a bachelor's degree from Princeton University and a master's from the University of Washington. She currently lives in Seattle.

Photograph by Don Wilson ©

www.AnneLipscomb.com

Printed in the United States
152728LV00002B/79/P